Today is the first day of
the rest of your life

Today Is the First Day of the Rest of Your Life

Robert Thomas Allen

Cartoons by Andy Cienik

McClelland and Stewart Limited

© 1971 by Robert Thomas Allen
Reprinted 1972, 1973
ALL RIGHTS RESERVED

0-7710-0955-0

Published with the co-operation of
The Canadian Life Insurance Association

The Canadian Publishers
McClelland and Stewart Limited
25 Hollinger Road, Toronto 374

Printed and bound in Canada

Contents

Preface *7*

1 Retirement's Public Image *11*
2 History Of Retirement *16*
3 Leisure – A Frightening Prospect *21*
4 Using Leisure Time Successfully *28*
5 Money *36*
6 Insurance And Pensions *48*
7 Employment *55*
8 To Move Or Not To Move *61*
9 Retirement In And Out Of Canada *71*
10 For Your Protection *85*
11 Health *93*
12 Living At Home *98*
13 Interests *103*

PREFACE

You might feel that a free-lance writer is as likely an author of a book on retirement as Mama Cass or Tiny Tim. But you're wrong. Hustling a living selling magazine articles is, in a sense, as far from being retired as you can get; yet a free-lancer's life has a lot of the ingredients of retirement, which, in essence, means being on your own, in charge of your own finances, free to make decisions, forced to survive psychologically without an office, factory routine, or work mates to bolster you up. Free-lance writing, like retirement, means having to have self-discipline. It means being able to work when nobody says you have to. It means being free to sleep-in until noon, or until next Tuesday, as far as anyone downtown cares; being able to have gin with your Rice Krispies, and a hang-over by lunch. It means being faced with the maddening experience of being free to choose the place where you're going to live, and it means having it left squarely up to you whether anybody needs you or not.

In this sense I've been retired for twenty-five years, and I've survived it all, including the day I quit a good salaried job to make my own way as a writer. I had the farewell party in the company cafeteria; and stepped out into the snow, one hand clutching the office gift (Taverner's *Birds of Eastern Canada*), the other my stomach, which was sinking down to my knees at the thought of being on my own, cut off from the human race like a shoplifter. The snow, the air, the clouds looked different than they had when I'd gone to work that morning, still under the benevolent protection of the country's economic structure.

Since then I've wandered into offices where I used to work, looking for someone to talk to after working at home by myself for three straight weeks. I would clutch old cronies by the sleeve and try to get them to go out for coffee with me, like the ancient mariner button-holding the wedding guest. I've budgeted an income a lot more unpredictable than yours will be when you retire, and I've been a lot more broke than you'll ever be, with no pension or union to fall back on.

I've done most of the things you're going to do when you retire and are probably talking about now. I've sold my house and moved to a warm climate and come back home in a blizzard. I've moved to farms and villages and beaches and apartments. I've lived with retired people and have been mistaken for them and I've talked to a lot of them. I've talked to retired beet farmers from Leamington, Ontario, and retired public relations men from Montreal and retired railway men from Winnipeg. We've stood talking outside lonely motels, our pant legs flapping in the breeze of passing transports; and leaning against hot car fenders outside desert gift shops; and peering at pelicans on the Atlantic, and at beach bums on the Pacific. I've lived in parts of this continent where retired people go and have seen men who took retirement so hard that they were ready to be wrapped in a plaid shawl and fed warm milk, and who just sat around on those green sidewalk benches donated by your friendly businessmen's association with Rest-A-While lettered on the back, and I've met others who were busier, happier, and making more dough than they had made before they retired. I've talked to men who were too busy, and enjoying themselves too much, to have noticed what it was like to be retired; and I've watched others play shuffleboard (dead man's pool) in those golf caps with little green windows at the back. I've stuck my nose into old yellow stucco chamber-of-commerce community halls that smelled of mould and Spanish moss, where they served instant coffee in paper cups that tasted as if it had been syphoned off a lagoon at low tide, and stood reading bulletin-board notices about meetings of the Sunshine Club and the Golden Age Club and the Hustler's Committee and Bingo on Friday with a film on "Inside the Bamboo Curtain" by someone with an unbelievable name, like Alma D'Artagnan. The last time I did this, a tough looking broad with white hair and long blue earrings sitting at a desk in the corner butted a cigarette and asked me if I wanted to join their Harvest Years Group, and I made a silent vow that the only way anybody would get me into a Harvest Years Club was if I were stuck in a wheelchair and someone cut the cables and started me rolling downhill for the clubhouse door.

In the meantime, I can tell you of a few mistakes I've seen retired people make, and of a few things to start thinking about now, in plenty of time for your own retirement.

"I haven't noticed any difference yet."

CHAPTER I:
RETIREMENT'S PUBLIC IMAGE

One danger in writing about retirement is that just treating it as a special subject tends to make it sound like a unique condition, like, say, a case of hives. There's already too much of this kind of writing, like those little items in the staff paper which are written in a kind of brisk, rustling prose that makes you think of starched white uniforms and back rubs. "No rocking chair for retired accountant Bill Easton, formerly Business Manager, Paint Division," a cut-line announces under a shot of old Bill in a ski cap looking up from pruning his petunias.

The way retirement is dealt with today, it's a wonder anybody has the spirit left to *grow* petunias, let alone prune them. Retired people are shown in those Sunday-supplement pictures where all the colour plates have slipped, sitting on screened porches in Havasu City, Arizona, looking stuffed, or holding highball glasses on boats on Biscayne Bay looking as if they could be towed out to sea without even noticing it. Whenever these pictures appear, the cut-line says "retired doctor" or "retired automobile worker," as if naming a certain blood type, or ailment. It's like saying "Ed Meadows, who has varicose veins."

Special courses now outline how to survive retirement, and there are even courses on how to organize courses on how to survive retirement, by eminent doctors and sociologists, with bibliographies as long as your arm. There's an American Association of Retired Persons (people who like to organize things never give up) and magazines for retired people, in which, sprinkled in among articles on topics like the last of the sailing ships, are useful facts about removal of the prostate gland, suggestions for some really great retirement jobs, like night watchman or basket weaver, and "How To" articles, like "How Not to Fall."

Newspaper columnists are firmly convinced that retirement is connected with ailing faculties. Last February, a retirement column in the Daytona Beach *Evening News*, called "Life Begins at 40," was giving advice on how retired people buying a house should choose one with no thresholds, hand grips around the bathtub, and non-skid floors in the hobby room. The same issue carried the story of the return to earth of Apollo 14 which carried Alan Shepard, who, at forty-seven, was just three years younger than the age at which many people retire. The previous day, the same retirement column was answering questions about diseases of the aged, while the front page carried the story of a grandfather of fifty-five with the wonderful name of Iggy Katona who had driven a tomato-red and mustard-yellow Dodge at an average speed of 152.5 miles an hour to win the Daytona 300, wearing cowboy boots.

The literature on retirement, by and large, gets more depressing the more cheerful it tries to be. "The final plateau," "afternoon frontiers," "What is this nonsense about 'The Hell of Being Sixty?'" "The Harvest Years," are a few phrases selected at random from material mimeographed both sides on soft paper that several people sent me when they heard I was writing about retirement. The eighteen-year-old daughter of a friend of mine must have been reading the same material. Just out of curiosity I asked her what she thought of retirement, and she said, "Imagine not being able to run and jump any more," already connecting retirement with geriatrics.

All this is having its effect. People are becoming scared of retirement. Northern Electric of Canada, after a survey on what they referred to as "the retirement experience," a phrase with overtones like "root-canal therapy," reported that the most frequent request from employees was for "counselling." Interviewers, sent around to find out why the employees hadn't answered the questionnaire, found "regrettable procrastination through dread or a timorous bravado," conjuring visions of a sulking mechanic peering at his lathe pretending there was nobody sitting beside him with a pad and sharp pencil.

Doctor Wilder Penfield, formerly Director of the Montreal Neurological Institute, wrote of a hysterical state called "false senility," brought about by compulsory retirement, being handed a watch, and told to take a "well-earned rest." The retiree next notices that he can't remember his license number (although he can remember the time his brother jumped on his stomach in 1911), and he thinks, by God I'm going dotty.

Many people are convinced that retirement brings about death. "You know, he'd only been retired six months when he died." One retired man told me, "I haven't noticed any difference yet," as if waiting for the anaesthetic to come out of a tooth. Another told me he got drunk the first night he retired and phoned his boss and asked him when he wanted him to start work again. He was sobered up considerably when his boss said, "Monday." He went back to work but by now he was so convinced that he shouldn't be working, that he felt as if he'd got out of bed against the doctor's orders, and he got an ulcer and had to retire again. One gent looked up at me from a deck chair, shaded his eyes from the sun, and said he had been retired for three years, two months, five weeks, two days and seven hours. He looked at his watch and added with a smile, "and forty minutes," as if surprised that he hadn't died yet. All the while his wife kept saying, "I tell him not to think of it," the way you'd tell someone to get his mind off an operation. A grey-haired widow of a railway engineer from Hamilton said, with a confused bit of logic, that it might sound heartless and anyone who knew her would know she didn't mean it that way but it was a mercy her husband died because he never would have survived retirement.

This gloomy public image has added to the shock of forced retirement. The trend is to lower the retirement age – some companies now compel retirement at fifty – and to many people it's a real psychological jolt. Whether compulsory retirement at *any* fixed age is a good thing is still a point of controversy. Those in favour of compulsory retirement claim that older people obstruct modernization and stand in the way of the promotion of the young. They also claim that compulsory retirement is a way of getting rid of people who lose efficiency with age, that it's more civilized than simply firing them, which of course, it is. If everyone has to retire at a certain age, it can't be taken too personally.

But opponents of compulsory retirement, and there are many, object to it on the grounds that actual age in years has no fixed relation to mental and physical age. When is a person old? Just lumping a person with a group of the same age ignores just about everything that makes him an individual human being: his attitudes, capacities, his very rate of aging.

But whether or not you agree with the principle of forced retirement, the fact is it's here and gaining acceptance, and your concern is how to make it work for you. Early retirement can mean an earlier start at another career, at a course of study, at many things you've wanted to do. The fact that it's compulsory, and the retirement age fixed, means that you have plenty of warning and plenty of time to start making your plans.

CHAPTER 2: HISTORY OF RETIREMENT

Retirement is not a kind of unavoidable misfortune. It's an economic fact. It's part of the economic structure of modern life, an outcome of a well-heeled society. My youngest daughter, at twenty-seven, has just retired on her own savings to spend a year and a half in Europe. A young assistant manager of a branch bank told me the other day that he thought the time was coming when people wouldn't retire suddenly at the age of, say, fifty-five; they'd retire one year out of every five all their lives. Retirement is no longer connected with disrupted life processes, age, ill health, or abandonment, any more than are income taxes or immigration laws.

It's now an important phase of life to each of us, and it's becoming increasingly important to the nation, as the retired population increases. In the 1900's it was rare for a man to quit a job while he could still work. Today most employers require their workers to retire at sixty-five, and often they offer optional retirement at sixty-two or sixty. Under union regulations, automobile workers can retire at sixty-two on full pension and at fifty-five, on reduced pension. People are retiring earlier and living longer.

Leisure has had a peculiar history. The man who is retired today is a rare and strange fowl in terms of past ages. In an article in the *Imperial Oil Review*, June Callwood, the Canadian journalist, remarks on the paradox that now that leisure, which has been idealized for so many centuries, has actually arrived, it's a threat to man's happiness. Man has been conditioned for so long to feel guilty if he's not working that he finds leisure "scary open ground." "For this reason, the continent's favourite leisure pastimes are different techniques for hiding, for being less conscious. They include drinking, sleep, sex, television, eating, trivial conversation and watching athletes." It is pointed out in this article that it was a suspiciously convenient coincidence that along with the Industrial Age came the Calvanist doctrine that work is noble and leisure the devil's opportunity. H. G. Wells puts "the fall," – when man forgot how to play – further back, to the age of agriculture, "the onset of foresight, that is." In *The Outline of Man's Work and Wealth*, he writes: "Man . . . is not by nature a toiler; toil is a phase in his development; he has had to be subdued to toil, and whenever an excuse appears, cheerfulness breaks through."

The advent of agriculture changed all this. Ordinary life in cultivating communities throughout history has been a life of continuous labour. There was a lot of leisure among certain classes in Rome, with free time for horsing around in public baths. According to one theory there's always been a leisure class. "The everyday work of getting a livelihood is the exclusive occupation of the inferior class. This inferior class includes slaves and other dependents, and ordinarily also all the women," says Thorstein Veblen in *The Theory of the Leisure Class*, writing of early Icelandic communities. "Employments [of men of the upper classes] are government, warfare, religious observances and sports." But after the collapse of Rome any special centres of leisure disappeared.

In the later great European civilizations "holy days" had not yet become holidays. In France, around 1700 – that is, not long after the time when, in Canada, La Salle was making expeditions out of what is now Kingston, Ontario, for the Mississippi – there were eighty-four workless days; but they weren't days when you didn't have to work, they were days when work was taboo, something like Victorian Sundays. H. G. Wells notes that it was only in centres where there were mixtures of people, with gypsy types and vestiges of the old nomads, that holy days became holidays during which men indulged in some of their favourite pastimes – bull fights, horse races, foot races, dancing, and getting plastered. "It is quite a delusion," Wells writes, "to think that the past was a leisurely time and that this is a driving time. The past was a time of almost universal drudgery and insufficiency."

Things got worse before they got better. Constant drudgery in factories for men, women, and children became the usual thing. In *Hard Times*, a book of documents of the Industrial Revolution in Britain, E. Royston Pike states that the children often began work in textile mills at six years of age, and sometimes five, and usually worked fourteen hours a day and sometimes fifteen or sixteen. Kids working in flax mills were kept at it by being flogged with straps; they were fined if they were caught combing their hair or washing themselves on company time. When a woman worked topless it meant something different than it does now. It meant she worked in a hot, wet coal pit, pulling cars of coal on all fours by a chain attached to a belt around her waist.

But in the meantime, increasing numbers of more prosperous people were beginning to enjoy a bit of the leisure that, in the next hundred years, culminated in today's affluent, easy age of paid holidays, travel, and retirement. It's something mankind has worked and fought for down through the ages. Retirement, in the sense of freedom from compulsory toil, is in the main stream of human progress, and the man who, facing retirement today, regards it as a calamity, should remind himself that most of man's great achievements were accomplished during time off from the business of making a living – during periods of productive leisure.

"What do you do when you've polished both cars?"

CHAPTER 3: LEISURE – A FRIGHTENING PROSPECT

Freedom from prescribed toil is a relatively recent and still unfamiliar experience, perhaps all the more frightening because workers have come such a long way in the past forty years. Conditions have improved to the point where a job means comfort, security, friendship, lots of jolly times at the Jiffy Lunch wagon or sitting around the company coffee shop. In any of the jobs at lower income levels it's almost impossible to get fired now, no matter how inept you are, or how indifferent to the welfare of the company. Everybody gets holidays with pay, and they're getting longer. The forty-hour week is being shortened.

No wonder people are frightened of retirement. It's like being dumped out of the cradle. Retirement is the beginning of responsibility, of being on your own. It means being on your own feet for the first time since you began work, of having an expanded experience, of being able to choose where you want to live instead of being nice and tidy and snug and bolted down by Big Brother in one place. It means the freedom to make a decision (nothing is harder on the mind). It means experiences that are stranger to most men than a walk on the moon, like living at home with their wives all day.

It means the shock of suddenly being able to do what you've been dreaming of doing and talking of doing during those socked-in winter mornings when you sat around the coffee shop watching the waitresses picking up their orders from under those brass warming lights, like maidens around the vestal hearth, dreaming out loud to your cronies. "What a day! You know what I'm going to do as soon as I retire? I'm going to get a nice little South Sea island with nothing but pelicans around me." It means putting your money where your mouth was; and finding yourself on the beach of your imagination, looking at real pelicans, getting agoraphobia, and realizing that the best way to retire to a South Sea island is in your imagination.

Retirement means suddenly finding yourself in that quaint little village you used to drive through on Sundays, when you'd say to your wife, "This is where I'd like to live when I retire," and knowing that you now are stuck with the realization that you *can* live there. It's the shock of suddenly not having any excuse for not being happy. It means being in the position of a group of automobile workers in Windsor who were interviewed about retirement by the Toronto *Globe and Mail*, who, when they referred to their former jobs, sounded like released prisoners of war ("It was like being in jail; they had guards on the gate") or like characters out of Dostoevsky ("I no longer have to get up and trudge off through the snow and slush") but they all had peculiar expressions on their faces as they peered out of the pages of the *Globe and Mail*, as if someone had called their bluff and they were looking down long vistas of contented years at what the Canadian Older Workers Branch of the Manpower Utilization Branch describes as "a period of well-deserved contentment."

If there's anything unnerving in this world it's being suddenly handed what you want, for instance all the time in the world to spend at that hobby you always wished you had the time to stay with, like writing your memoirs. There you are, suddenly with no reason why you can't stay with it, and you suddenly notice that a blank sheet of paper looks a lot more blank than it was when you would have written wonderful things on it except that you had to go to work. I've known several men who were going to write books if they ever had the time. "If I told the story of my life nobody would believe it," they often said over their shoulders, hurrying to an appointment. I finally pinned one man down who had been saying this to me for years. When I asked him how far he'd got with his book now that he was retired, I found that the dramatic things he had been hinting at these years and which made him sound like a cross between the Marquis de Sade and Candy's father, consisted of (a) owning an apartment building once in Pittsburgh, and (b) running a nurses' uniform shop in Montreal.

Retirement doesn't mean a retreat from life, or becoming unplugged, like TV. It means the sudden acquisition of more life. It's this that some people find hard to handle. I remember one time at a small flying field in British Columbia hearing a young man in blue pullover and beige bermudas, who was apparently retired and putting in time watching the planes, calling out to a friend, "What do you do when you've polished both cars?" I gathered from his tone and expression that he was only partly joking.

But the freedom of choice of activities and the widening of the scope of life is the very thing that makes retirement, for others, an adventure – a chance to get back to the world the way it was before they got into the rut of hustling a living, when they were young and unjaded enough to notice the world, smell it, feel it through their pores and nerve ends. Every time I come across one of those Sunday supplement items with some title like "The Senior Scene," showing a former petroleum executive, seventy-five, of Swift River, Alberta, sitting on a fibre-glass cruiser on a fibre-glass lake in Arizona, I wish I could sneak up on him with some fourth-dimensional snorkle outfit and tow him back through time to the world of his youth when the sun glinted off the sea oats and a lake was a wild, secret, magic place of mud, hot pine needles, swamps, woodsmoke, algae, and the thump of an oar on a still summer morning; when a boat was an irresistible device that smelled of bullrushes and hot planks and enabled you to sit on top of the water without getting wet and peer down into a world of sunfish, minnows, weeds, and mystery; and you could lie on your back in it and drift till you heard a soft scratching sound and looked up to find you'd drifted into some reeds with a dragon fly waving above you in the gentle morning breeze against a white cloud, like a windsock pointing the way to the future.

There's no scarcity of stories of people for whom retirement meant lively and productive second careers. In a booklet published by Mutual Benefit Life Insurance Company, Ray Giles tells of a man named Frederick Wolcott Dearing, who, at the age of seventy-two, after thirty years as an accountant, became an ordained priest of the Episcopal Church. He also tells of Dr. Lillien J. Martin, who, when she was retired from Stanford University at sixty-five, became consulting psychologist, then opened a pre-school children's clinic, then a clinic for people over fifty. She learned to drive at seventy-eight, learned Spanish and typing at eighty-eight and took off on a 20,000-mile trip around South America.

Many great figures of history made their greatest contributions to mankind after the age at which we face retirement today. You might not approve of what some of them did. You might not like them at all, but you can't deny that they were flourishing and active and interested in life in the latter part of their lives. Eisenhower became Supreme Commander of the Allied Powers in Europe at sixty, and President of the United States at sixty-three. Churchill at seventy-nine was too busy to go to Stockholm to accept the Nobel Prize for literature. Plato wrote the Theatetus when he was sixty and was working on the Laws at eighty. The great eighteenth-century French writer, Voltaire, was arrested for needling Frederick of Prussia at the age of sixty and wrote *Candide*, one of his chief works, at sixty-five. Verdi composed two of his greatest operas between seventy-four and eighty.

One of the most interesting people I've known personally who is still going strong far past usual retirement age is a man I met when I wrote an article for *Maclean's* magazine on a Greek cruise – an Oxford graduate who had been professor of classics at the University of Calgary, Alban D. Winspear. He got the idea of conducting cruises on chartered Greek fishing boats when he was fifty-nine, and a few years later had organized funds and had his own boat built in a shipyard near Athens – a seventy-five-foot motor yacht called the *Lysistrata*. He began informally shepherding shore trips to archaeological sites and giving the paying passengers classical lectures, which he called "deck talks." Winspear, seventy when I met him, was a man at work, and he was thoroughly involved. He's a tall man whose expression alternates between a rather terrifying owlish stare and a pleasant boyish grin. Beneath a stratosphere of scholarships, he has roots in Alberta where he spent much of his life, and the result of this mixed background was that he would switch from quoting poetry, which he does as naturally as a shriner tells jokes, to belting out a solo of "Home on the Range" in full view of Mount Parnassus. He accompanied the passengers on their evening strolls around town, wearing a yachting cap, smoking Papastratos cigarettes, ordering ouzo, the powerful Greek aperitif, speaking a courtly Greek to the waiters. He'd sit there reading from Thucydidies on the Spartan-Athenian wars, with the same breeze that confounded the Corinthian fleet unravelling his white hair like loose ends of a ball of string – every inch a man involved in an important work. The last time I saw him, he had taken off from the port of Eleusis to fly to London where he was getting involved in a third career, some abstruse computerized method of establishing the authenticity of the Epistles of Plato.

"Activities should create excitement and even tension."

CHAPTER 4: USING LEISURE TIME SUCCESSFULLY

The success of retirement, according to sociologists, is proportional to the amount of planning. The planning itself is important. It should be done just the way you'd plan a year in Europe, or the opening of a new business, and in the same spirit.

One expert recommends that retirement objectives should be written down methodically and deliberately and worked over and changed and hacked at, just like a good manuscript. Don't try to make the outline neat and tidy and just the right length. All editors know that the awful manuscripts are always just the right length and beautifully spaced, and theatrical producers know that the dull plays always end right on time.

Doctor Wilfred G. Scott, a psychologist and an employment specialist, recommends that you should talk over your past accomplishments, your interests and ambitions and retirement plans with your wife and friends. He says that talking about it will help you clarify for yourself what you want to do. "The leisure years offer an exciting future to those who prepare for them."

Doctor Scott uses the word "leisure" here, incidentally, to mean freedom from the old job, not to mean doing nothing, for he strongly urges keeping active. "It is necessary for us to retain our sense of usefulness. We must remain active. We must remain useful. We must still accomplish things. If you bind your arm to your body and fail to use it, it withers and becomes useless. We call this atrophy through disuse. It is true not only of the arm but true of ourselves. We must retain our sense of usefulness to the world or we become atrophied." One thing Doctor Scott stresses is to take no notice of the myth that our learning capacity wanes as we get older. "Older people are their own worst enemies. They say, 'Of course, I haven't the memory I once had, I haven't the ability I had when I was younger,' so many people have told them that they are slow that they believe it, and it requires discussion to assure them that they are quite as good at learning as they ever were."

There's been a lot of interesting research on what happens to our capacity to learn as we get older. Most established attitudes are turning out to be as unfounded as some of man's early ideas about pregnancy, like the early Greek belief that women brought it on by turning their backs to the North Wind. (One woman I mentioned this to said she believed that too, but it depended on who was standing toward the south.) For instance, it's now medically established that the brain doesn't wear out. The brain is subject to physiological mishaps like any other part of the body, but it doesn't wear out, like piston rings or upholstery, as many people think it does.

Doctor Penfield says that normally after sixty the brain is actually ready for its best performance in some fields. A Columbia University experimenter found that older people could learn Russian, a tough language, just as fast as the young, providing they were interested. Tests show that older people shine in linguistics, which is at the heart of intellect and inseparable from thought. An article on this by Dr. James B. Stroud, Professor of Education and Psychology, College of Education, State University of Iowa, has been reprinted by the Canadian Department of Manpower and Immigration. Doctor Stroud writes: "I suppose one may become so old that he drops the verbs from his sentences, or modifies adjectives with nouns, but I have not seen such a person. Man's handwriting, his spelling, his diction, his employment of syntax, stands up remarkably well ... his vocabulary is adequate to sustain his intellectual life. We all know what it means to walk and move about like a man of sixty-five or seventy. If there are peculiarities in speech and thought that distinguish him from a man of forty, they seem less obvious. All this takes on significance when we realize that language is the heart and centre of intellectual life. It is the most highly generalized skill that man has acquired...."

The vital relationship of speech and thought is described by A.A. Luce, professor of logic at Trinity College, Dublin. "Because he [man] is a rational spirit, he thinks; because he is a rational spirit in a living body he utters ('outers') his thoughts. Discourse is neither speechless thought, nor thoughtless speech." (The reason the young talk the way they do, by the way, is not simply just to be in fashion. It's because they don't know what they're talking about. I once asked eight people what I would mean if I said, "That's my bag," and I got eight different answers, all worse than the question, including, "You'd mean you'd groove it.")

One day on a flight to Montreal, an air-conditioner salesman sitting next to me, who was intrigued by my job as a free-lance writer, told me I should claim depreciation on my brain, which, he said, suffered from wear and tear just like sprinkler systems or escalators (Class 3, 5% on the Canadian Capital Cost Allowance form). It was about the only deduction I haven't tried on my income tax, but the fact is that the brain doesn't wear out. I read the other day of a theory that people wear out unevenly, and that their interests should be rotated like the tires on a car, and the author suggested that for this reason we should have many hobbies and interests. These analogies to tires and plumbing have to be watched when we're speaking of that mysterious, magic mechanism the human brain.

The idea of hobbies has to be watched too. The word has changed its meaning. It originally meant an obsession with some pursuit, like dog-breeding or photography. Now it usually applies to things that haven't even got a firm grip on the mind. People with "many interests and hobbies" are often desperately stuffing time with things like taking brass rubbings, bird watching, and making little roosters out of white pine or model boats out of bottle tops. There's nothing wrong with these activities in themselves. I'm a bird watcher from way back and I could probably easily become a brass rubber, but these mild and tentative pursuits that just involve a few of our faculties, although restful and beneficial for short periods, just as it's beneficial to have a snooze in a hammock, have nothing to do with the kind of activity that's needed for retirement. It's hard to define the difference between a hobby and a genuine interest. Perhaps a lack of self-consciousness. Thomas Carlyle wrote that when we were young, "We knew not that we had limbs, we only lifted, hurled and leapt." There's a difference between a person "having interests" and being so interested he doesn't even know he has interests.

Miss L. Wilson of the Department of Social Welfare, the Province of Saskatchewan, has some pertinent things to say on the quality of activity. "If your hobby when you retire is sitting at home alone tatting or weaving or doing leather work, these hobbies in themselves will not serve as a substitute, for they do not provide for human contacts nor do they have social value. If, on the other hand, through these hobbies are done alone, one extends their use to participation and sharing of the results in craft sales, exhibits, teaching of others – in other words if they result in human contacts and social values this is another matter.... A hobby should have the element of providing new ideas, new pleasures and new experiences and should give people an opportunity not to kill time but to live it...." She says that activities should create excitement and even tension. They should stimulate emotions and provide a zest for life. They should be intellectually and physically stimulating. "Retirement should never spell complete cessation of activity. Rather it should merely be a shift of activity to something which is voluntary and controllable, rather than compulsory and continuous.... Interviews with men and women nearing retirement have shown that their major needs are 'still being of use to people,' and 'still being part of things going on in the world.' "

One point made by Miss Wilson I can comment on from experience: "Retirement should never spell complete cessation of activity." The greatest mistake in the world is thinking that retirement means doing nothing. I've lived on streets in the south on which almost everyone was retired and doing nothing but enjoying what the Department of Manpower and Immigration refers to as "freedom from the responsibilities and pressure of the working world," and you've never seen such busy people. They thought up some of the damndest things to occupy themselves and satisfy their latent emotions. One widow used to rake her driveway every night so it would show up the footprints of some tall man she said came and peered into her window after she went to bed. Finding no footprints didn't discourage her either. "Well, he wasn't here last night," she'd call cheerfully across a yucca bush next morning.

This was in the days when a lot more flying saucers were visiting us earth people than there are now, and there was considerable interest in astral affairs. One man used to talk to people on Venus, with the help of some recording device and a medium in Daytona Beach. He had dozens of tapes of conversations he'd had with Venusians, relayed through the medium. He played one for me one noon hour.

"I hear," the Venusian said, speaking through the medium's thin, high-pitched, quavering voice, "that you have something on earth – something – eees eeet a nuclayyerr bomb?...." There was a certain modesty about this Venusian, and he always made it clear that he didn't know everything.

"Who knows whether he's right or not," the people on the street used to say. "I'll believe anything since they invented TV." (The logic behind this argument for accepting absolutely anything has always escaped me.)

One time when things were kind of quiet on Venus, we all started looking for a young man in a long white dinner jacket who ran along our street crouched over on dark nights – or so several retired people said. It had all the overtones of an early Hitchcock movie. I don't know how it started, or how I got swept up in the general hysteria, but for a while there, after supper on moonless nights, we all started wandering around with flashlights. "Who's that?" you'd say, shining your flashlight in a neighbour's face, who would look into the beam suspiciously and flash his light on *your* face. "Look at that!" some retired gent would shout suddenly making you jump. "God damn it, you can't tell me that anybody who runs crouched over like that in a long white coat is up to any good!" We'd all peer between the palm trees for this mysterious figure, whom nobody ever got a good look at, and finally all wander off a bit sheepishly, but still not convinced it was just nerves.

It caused a kind of tension around the street. There was one very un-retired family with a little boy who was always biting his sister, a curly-haired little girl who could let out blood-curdling screams that were startling enough any time, but in the present mood of the neighbourhood froze everyone as if someone had suddenly announced the discontinuation of green stamps, "I know what I'd do with *that* one if she belonged to me," retired mothers said.

Even the cats of the neighbourhood were affected. You couldn't quite describe it, but they all seemed excited and their hair stood out straight, and old eunuchs challenged hardened tom cats full of scars and sand spurs. They were always looking off into the distance, as if they saw something which would soon reach the street. They sat up in the shoes of the cabbage-palms yowling in the moonlight, and you'd see them running low and silently for the palmetto scrub. They chased one another like bad dreams with their tails out straight, and sat on hot sandy roads looking into one another's faces about six inches apart. Then you wouldn't see any cats around for two or three months.

Everyone needs to do nothing for short periods, but they should be very short. If man has nothing to do he'll find something, even if it means helping along his own disintegration. My only other comment on Miss Wilson's remarks on hobbies is that I don't think the social aspects are important to everyone. There are lots of people in this world who have been loners all their lives, and they're not going to change after retirement. But I think a hobby, to really mean anything, should be related to the work, history, and knowledge of man. Identifying stars for instance, is a mildly interesting pursuit that might occupy one hour out of every twenty-four. Astronomy, on the other hand, is an engrossing full-time study. Making a sun dial from a diagram in a hobby book is simply an exercise in home carpentry. Understanding how a sundial tells time, why the dial-face is marked out the way it is, involves basic astronomical laws and many of the great deductions of man. A hobby is what you make it: it can be a superficial occupation or a substantial and lasting interest.

"Retired workers will get along financially . . . if their income is greater than their expenses."

CHAPTER 5: MONEY

Much of the literature on the economics of retirement is unreadable stuff, and some is downright foolish. One report, for instance, from a University of Chicago course on retirement concludes: "Retired workers will get along financially in retirement if their income is greater than their expenses." Still, whether you work it out on an IBM computer or on the back of a book of bar matches, getting some idea of how you'll stand financially is the first step in planning retirement. There are dozens of ways of doing it, but what they all boil down to is figuring out as closely as you can what your *monthly* income and *monthly* expenses will be. A pamphlet entitled *The Subject is Money*, put out by the Life Insurance Companies in Canada, deals with retirement income so clearly and simply that it has been reprinted here, along with blank spaces for you to fill in.

YOU EARN A LOT OF MONEY

You've probably been working for quite a few years now. And it's likely you're earning more money than you ever expected to – a fact that becomes all too clear every April.

Did you ever wonder just how much money you'll earn in your lifetime? Have you ever sat down to figure it out?

Try it. It may be an eye opener.

First, estimate how much money you've earned since you left school.

UP TO NOW, I'VE EARNED $_____

Now, figure out how much money you'll probably earn between now and your retirement age.

BETWEEN NOW AND MY RETIREMENT, I'LL PROBABLY EARN $_____

SO DURING MY WORKING YEARS I'LL EARN A TOTAL OF ABOUT $_____

Adds up to a small fortune, doesn't it?

Don't be surprised. It's not at all unusual for a man to earn between a quarter and half a million dollars in his lifetime. And you're no exception.

HOW WELL DO YOU HANDLE YOUR MONEY?

It's not so much what you *earn* but what you *keep* that's the yardstick of how well you manage your money. Or rather, how much you invest safely and profitably.

Who is really better off? The man who earns $15,000 a year and saves $500, or the man earning $10,000 who saves $1,000?

In these terms, how do you measure up?

Why not figure it out now?

Ask yourself: How much of the money I've earned since I left school have I managed to keep? What is the total of my financial assets: saving accounts, equity in my home or other real estate, cash values in my life insurance, stocks and bonds? (Leave out your employer or personal pension plan for now. We'll get to that later.)

UP TO NOW I'VE SAVED $_____

How does this total compare to your earnings?

What percentage of the money you've earned so far in your life have you kept for yourself and your family?

MY SAVINGS ARE_____ PER CENT OF MY EARNINGS
$_____

If it's rather low, don't be surprised. It's the exceptional man who, on top of his pension plan savings, has managed to keep more than ten per cent of his total earnings.

HOW MUCH MONEY WILL BE IN YOUR ESTATE?

Most men have only a vague idea of what they'd be worth if they were to die today. How about you?

Here's one way to figure it out.

As you did on the previous page, total up your savings accounts, equity in your home or other real estate, stocks and bonds. But this time include the value of any employer or personal pension plan benefits payable on death. And instead of the cash values in your life insurance, you now write in the *face value* of your policies – that is, the sums payable on death – plus any accumulated dividends.

IF I WERE TO DIE TODAY, THE TOTAL VALUE OF MY ESTATE
WOULD BE APPROXIMATELY $_____

What does this mean to your wife and children?

The total dollar value of your estate is important, of course. But the crucial consideration is how much *income* it will provide for your family, and for how long.

Let's estimate that your estate could earn six per cent per

year. This is realistic. It's possible that your family could get more income – say, by using up some of the capital – but this is by no means certain. At six per cent, *each $1,000* in your estate will provide income of *$5 a month* for your family.

AT $5 A THOUSAND, MY ESTATE WOULD GIVE MY FAMILY A MONTHLY INCOME OF $_____

* Survivor's benefits from the Canada and Quebec Pension Plans will provide a widow with an additional monthly income. Example: If a husband had earnings of $5,400 or more, the monthly income of his widow with two dependent children would be about $123; with three children, about $150, as of January 1, 1971.

GOVERNMENT PENSION PLAN SURVIVOR'S BENEFITS WOULD PROVIDE A MONTHLY INCOME OF ABOUT $_____

Add these figures and you have the amount of monthly income your family would have to live on if you died today.

THUS, MY FAMILY'S TOTAL MONTHLY INCOME WOULD BE ABOUT $_____

Is it enough? Only you and your wife can answer that question.

We know from experience, however, that even though a man's estate may seem adequate when looked on as a total amount, it's often too small when viewed in terms of monthly income.

IN RETIREMENT, WILL MONEY BE A PROBLEM?

Chances are you're going to live to old age. Now is the time to plan for that day.

Will you be able to live comfortably in retirement? will you be able to afford the trips, the hobbies and the extras you'd like? Or will you have to watch every penny? Here's how you can answer these questions:

Above, you calculated the percentage of your earnings that you've managed to save up to the present time. If you continue to save at that rate, how much money will you have on the day you retire?

Simply multiply your *estimated total life-time earnings* by the *per cent* of your savings.

IN MY LIFETIME, I'LL EARN ABOUT [SEE ABOVE]
$_____

IF I CONTINUE TO SAVE AT MY PRESENT RATE OF [SEE ABOVE]
PER CENT _____, AT AGE 65 I'LL HAVE ABOUT
$_____

This is your total dollar worth at retirement. But what does this mean in terms of your day-to-day life? What income will this give you to live on?

AT $5 PER THOUSAND, THIS AMOUNT OF MONEY WILL GIVE ME
AND MY WIFE A MONTHLY INCOME OF $_____

MY EMPLOYER OR PERSONAL PENSION PLAN WILL PAY A
MONTHLY INCOME OF ABOUT $_____

GOVERNMENT PENSION PLANS WILL PAY A MONTHLY INCOME
OF ABOUT $_____

*OLD AGE SECURITY WILL PAY A MONTHLY INCOME OF ABOUT
$_____

---

*The booklet gives some figures indicating what these may be, but explains that, as these benefits fluctuate with the cost of living, it is impossible to give exact amounts. To estimate the benefits you will receive, refer to Chapter 6, "Insurance and Pensions," which outlines the Canada Pension Plan, Old Age Security Pension, and Guaranteed Income Supplement.

THEREFORE, MY MONTHLY INCOME IN RETIREMENT WILL TOTAL ABOUT $_____

Is it enough?

Again, only you and your wife can answer the question.

It's not surprising that the booklet suggests that, if your financial picture doesn't look too good, you get in touch with your local insurance man, who will show you how you can improve things. This isn't a bad idea. Although some insurance salesmen have a habit of disappearing behind the iron curtain after they've signed you up for a policy, and leaving you to deal with a company robot, if you have a good insurance agent, as I happen to have, he can be a big help.

A typical plan for plotting retirement finances is given here:

Our Financial Resources for Retirement Years

RESOURCES	UPON RETIREMENT WILL PRODUCE	
	In cash and/or	In Monthly Income
Old Age Security Pension	$_____	$_____
Canada Pension Plan	$_____	$_____
Life Insurance (Total values in policies no longer needed for protection, which will produce cash or income)	$_____	$_____
Company or Union Pension or Retirement plan	$_____	$_____
Annuities, individually owned	$_____	$_____

Savings Accounts	$_____	$_____
Checking Accounts	$_____	$_____
Stocks, Bonds, Mutual Funds	$_____	$_____
Real Estate (market value or rent from home or other real estate)	$_____	$_____
Mortgages	$_____	$_____
Accounts and Notes Receivable	$_____	$_____

FOR INCOME WE WILL USE	EACH WILL PRODUCE MONTHLY
_____	$_____
_____	$_____
_____	$_____
_____	$_____

Total monthly income _____.

FOR CASH EMERGENCIES WE WILL KEEP	Amount
_____	$_____
_____	$_____
_____	$_____

Total Cash _____

FOR PROTECTION WE WILL KEEP
THIS LIFE INSURANCE:

Company name and policy number	Amount
_____	$_____
_____	$_____

Total Protection _____

OUR MONTHLY MONEY PLAN FOR RETIREMENT

PAYMENTS WE HAVE TO MEET	NOW	AFTER RETIREMENT
Rent or Mortgage	$_____	$_____
Other Housing Expenses (taxes, repairs, insurance, etc.)	$_____	$_____
Electricity, Heat, Gas, Water	$_____	$_____
Life Insurance	$_____	$_____
Health Insurance	$_____	$_____
Hospital Insurance	$_____	$_____

Other Insurance (auto, liability, etc.) $_____ $_____

Contributions $_____ $_____

Income Taxes $_____ $_____

Property and Local taxes $_____ $_____

Total Payments We Have To Meet

$_____ $_____

DAY-TO-DAY EXPENSES	NOW	AFTER RETIREMENT
Food	$_____	$_____
Clothing	$_____	$_____
Household Incidentals (laundry, cleaning, etc.)	$_____	$_____
Transportation and Work Expenses	$_____	$_____
Newspapers, Magazines, Recreation	$_____	$_____
Medicines and Dental and Optometrist	$_____	$_____
Personal Allowances	$_____	$_____
Total Day-to-Day Expenses	$_____	$_____

SUMMARY OF OUR RETIREMENT INCOME AND EXPENSES

(a) We expect this monthly income $_____

    We plan to use it this way:

    For payments we have to meet $_____

    For day-to-day expenses $_____

(b) Total Monthly Expenses $_____

The crucial point in all this calculating and listing and accounting is obviously the comparison of (a) and (b). If (b) is higher than (a) you have to start doing something about it. If you can't raise (a) you've got to cut down on (b) perhaps by cutting down on waste. The experts in these matters claim that nine out of ten families waste ten per cent or more of their income through careless management. They give as the main principles of correcting the situation: eliminating overbuying and getting more use out of clothing and appliances by taking proper care of them; buying more economically; in some cases buying second-hand things; shunning installment buying, which costs you money in interest; cutting down on income tax by learning about and taking advantage of all the legal deductions.

One important item to consider in your calculations is your car. Most people shy away from facing just how much a car costs. To get a realistic picture, add up the following main categories of costs:

Fixed or standing costs that go on whether or not your car is being driven. These costs include deprecation and insurance. A car costs you money just sitting in the garage. It's a sad commentary on modern merchandising but the condition in which you keep your car hasn't much effect on what it's worth. It depreciates because of fashion. One method of figuring the amount your car costs in depreciation is to depreciate a car starting with its new price 29 per cent each year, or $290 per thousand. It's estimated that a car depreciates between $800 and $1100 the first year whether it moves or not.

Running or variable costs vary according to the amount you drive, and include gas, oil, tires, routine maintenance costs such as lubrication, front-end alignments, brake relining, and tune-ups; and non-scheduled costs like plugged rads, cracked distributor caps, and pranged fenders.

Merle E. Dowd, a mechanical engineer and financial analyst for Ford, in a book entitled *How to Save Money When You Buy and Drive Your Car*, estimates that a Ford two-door with automatic transmission costs a total of $1,680 the first year, $1,307 the second . . . . $653 the tenth, with most of the decrease being due to lessening depreciation. This is an average of $937 every year to run your car, or in the neighbourhood of $75 a month, and only you and your wife can decide whether a car is worth that much to you. I know I never want to be without one as long as I live in North America.

"... and in a few years you can go to the finest college."

CHAPTER 6: INSURANCE AND PENSIONS

Although there's no necessary connection between life insurance and retirement, in practice there's generally a very strong one, because, for most of us, life insurance is the only kind of real saving we ever do, and it usually plays a basic part in retirement income. The Canadian Life Insurance Association puts out a booklet called "Life Insurance, a Canadian Handbook," which you can get by writing 44 King Street West, Toronto 1. It describes the principles behind insurance, gives a bit of its history, and explains the different kinds of insurance, which we all think we're familiar with, but are usually a bit vague about. The booklet has a special section on annuities, and gives half a dozen or more specific examples of how various kinds of life insurance arrangements work out, and how your life insurance can help take care of your retirement.

Whole Life Insurance ("one insures *against* something but is assured *of* it" – Fowler's *Modern English Usage*) is also called Straight Life or Ordinary Life. Primarily it provides protection but it also has a savings factor. All policies except term insurance have accumulated values. They're called nonforfeiture values because you don't forfeit them if, for instance, you stop paying premiums. Premiums on a Whole Life policy are paid throughout the policyholder's lifetime. On his death, it pays either a lump sum or an income to his beneficiary.

Endowment Insurance has a bigger savings factor than Whole Life (at greater cost) and is designed to provide a sizeable amount of money to cover some future event: a college education for your children, for example, or money for your own retirement.

The savings in insurance policies can be arranged in dozens of combinations and permutations. For instance, policies can be converted to paid-up reduced insurance for life; or paid-up full insurance for a limited period; or can be cashed or used to buy annuities.

Term Insurance gives you protection, and usually *only* protection: that is, there are no savings along with it for a given number of years (term of years).

An Annuity is a policy that deals with survival benefits instead of death benefits, and it's of special interest to anyone planning retirement. It pays a policyholder a certain income for the rest of his life. In the Canadian Handbook on life insurance, it is stated "People buy life insurance because of the possibility that they *may not live long enough* to support their dependents. People buy life annuities because of the possibility that they *may outlive* their earning period and need a steady income during their remaining years." Life insurance can be converted to annuities; that is, you don't take the money coming to you, but in return the insurance company will pay you so much a month as long as you live.

There are all kinds of shades and grades of annuities, too. A *straight life annuity* pays an income to the annuitant during his remaining lifetime, and stops when he dies. A *life annuity with instalments* pays an income for life, but if the policyholder dies within a guarantee period, the income payments are continued to a beneficiary for the balance of the guaranteed period. An *instalment refund annuity* pays an income to the annuitant for life. But if the annuitant dies before he has received as much money as he paid, the balance of the income payments are continued to his beneficiary until total income payments equal that amount. A *cash refund annuity* is the same except that the beneficiary gets a lump sum. The approximate cost for each $10 of monthly income for life, on a straight life annuity basis bought at the age of 65 and to begin immediately, is $1200. Annuity contracts are paid for and payable in various ways. An *immediate annuity* is paid for all at once with a single payment and the income starts a month later, if income payments are to be made monthly, or a year later if they're to be made annually. A *deferred annuity* provides income that will begin on some future date, and is paid either by a single payment or in instalments. This type of annuity, which provides cash surrender value and loan privileges and some insurance, is a *retirement annuity*, to which various companies give various names.

One of the most important changes in life insurance today is that insurance companies now offer what are known as *variable contracts*, which are designed to allow policyholders to assume investment risk in return for the possibility of larger returns. Most of the major life insurance companies in Canada are now developing their versions of this kind of contract. One of the objectives of these contracts is to minimize the effects of possible future inflation. Economists call it creeping inflation, but it has moved fast enough to keep well ahead of government aids. The Old Age Security Pension, for example, was increased from $65 in 1962 to $80 in 1971, but because of the increased cost of living, this $80 buys only as much as $62 would have done in 1962.

The plans that insurance companies have come up with to

help you hedge against inflation are all based on the idea that investments supporting the policy are put in a special "segregated" fund which is invested wholly or partially in common stocks.

Since 1942 the cost of living has risen regularly each year. While the general trend for most common stocks has been to rise, their progress has had much more of an up-and-down quality. Annuitites can be handled as variable contracts, so that the value of the annuity payments goes up or down with the value of a particular portfolio on which it is based. The main objection to this kind of arrangement is that regardless of the mathematics, logic, or justice of the arrangement, people don't like the down part nearly as much as the up.

Any life insurance policy or annuity which has a savings feature can be registered with the Department of National Revenue, the premium, or a portion of it, deducted from taxable income when calculating income tax payments. There is, of course, a limit to the allowable deduction. It may be a help to you to consult your life insurance agent or company. They can handle this for you.

When you calculate your financial resources for retirement, the possible government aids you'll be concerned with are: the Canada Pension Plan, Old Age Security Pension, and Guaranteed Income Supplement.

The Canada Year Book gives all the details on these and you can get booklets on them from any Canada Pension Plan Office. Look up "Canada Pension Plan" in the phone book. You can also write to the Minister of National Health and Welfare for a statement of your Unadjusted Pensionable earnings credited to your Record of Earnings, providing you don't write more often than once a year.

Incidentally, if you haven't got into the habit of making use of government departments and publications, it's time you did. The government puts out information on just about everything, either free or in low-priced editions, and I've found federal and provincial government employees, by and large, gentle, civilized people who are helpful, friendly, informed, and under no compulsion to lean on you or put on an act to impress you. They know their stuff and are generally ready to talk to anyone on their particular subject.

You can get Canada Pension Plan payments at sixty-five if you're not making more than $990 a year. As you earn over that amount, the pension comes down. Over seventy you get your full pension anyway, no matter how much you make. Full retirement benefits under the Canada and Quebec Pension Plans will not become payable until 1976. If you start collecting before that, you receive a reduced amount. If you don't become eligible until 1976, and if your earnings are at or over the maximum pensionable (this "ceiling" has been raised, since the beginning of the plan, to $5,400 in 1971 and it may be raised again) you will receive 25% of your average monthly pensionable earnings. Based on the present (1971) ceiling this would be at least $112.50 a month. Canada Pension Plan benefits are payable whether you live in Canada or not; in other words, if you're qualified to get it, you can collect it while lounging around the Mediterranean if that's where you want to spend your retirement.

Old Age Security Pension is payable to anyone sixty-five or over. It amounts to $80 a month, and it's payable whether you work or not, and, of course, equal amounts are paid to both husband and wife. This can be increased by the Guaranteed Income Supplement, which is available to persons with low incomes. The amount of income determines the amount of the supplement. The maximum supplement is $95 a month for a married couple or $55 a month for a single person: i.e. a couple with no other income would receive $255 a month and a single person $135 a month. To collect Old Age Security Pension you have to have lived in Canada a total of forty years since the age of eighteen, or for ten years preceding application, or to have compensated for every year of absence during that ten years by two years spent in Canada before the ten years. All that being established, and assuming you qualify for the pension, if you've spent a total of twenty-five years in Canada, not necessarily consecutively, since you were twenty-one, you can collect your Old Age Pension outside Canada indefinitely. Otherwise, if you're away for more than six months, your Old Age Pension will be suspended until you come back.

There are other, and important benefits from these plans – not gone into here because they don't apply directly to the subject of this book, which is retirement – for instance: death benefits, widow's pension, orphans' benefits, which can amount to very substantial payments. These are dealt with in publications available, free, at Canada Pension Plan offices.

"I can out-think half the guys of thirty and outproduce them and outwork them."

CHAPTER 7: EMPLOYMENT

One thing you should face now is the possibility that you might want to, or have to, make extra money after you've retired. You'll probably be able to live on less than you're used to. You won't be bringing up a family, and, depending on what kind of life you live, you'll probably save on downtown meals and city transportation. But if your calculations show that, after all possible economy measures, your expenses are still going to be higher than your income, you may have to figure on part-time work.

In spite of anti-discrimination laws about turning people down because of their age, you won't find it as easy to get a job now as when you were twenty-three and full of juice and confidence. It's a cold experience to drop into an employment office when you're on the downward slope of life. I've done it. Every now and then when I got the wind up about supporting myself as a writer, I've dropped in on some office with a fancy name like Executive Placement Service Centre or Communications Industry Personnel Agency and have sat in the foyer like someone from under a toadstool, peering around a floral arrangement waiting to be noticed by a faintly hostile young receptionist who sat there obviously wishing someone would tell me to go away, and feeling as out of place as an old eel fisherman in a boutique, no good for anything besides the job I'd always worked at.

There are a few people who can handle this kind of thing without trouble. I know one man my age who can whip up a job any time he feels like it. He starts right in with, "Now don't give me any of that guff about being sixty. I can outthink half the guys of thirty on your staff, and outwork them and outproduce them and I have a lot more experience, so let's just not discuss it." But few of us can wind up this kind of self-confidence.

Some good advice is given by one course on retirement conducted by the University of Chicago. It's suggested that you'll feel a lot better if you go about looking for a job in a methodical way, beginning with writing a job summary – a short, concise statement of your background, with a brief listing of previous jobs – and being mentally prepared for some of the obvious questions: your age, the money you expect, and why you're looking for work, and whether you'll be willing to take less than you used to get. With a job summary you'll have all your facts at hand and won't get rattled when you have to fill out one of those senseless application forms that leave no room to write anything. Also, without something concrete to refer to during an interview, you may get rattled and forget things, like the name of the company where you used to work, or your wife's name; and the interviewer will probably be a young guy with long hair and one of those pearl button jackets (which before the word took on another meaning, we used to call reefers) who isn't too keen on talking to someone out of the mezolithic epoch like you anyway. Or worse still it may be someone your age in a pearl button jacket who will hate you for reminding him of how old he is. The thing is, in a pinch you can just attach your job history to the application and hand it to the interviewer, which will give you a chance to pull your thoughts together and steer the interview in the right direction and present your case in the best way possible. Another thing, you can make a lot of copies of your job history and circulate them.

You may have misgivings about applying for work when you're past retirement age. You may feel that the world has changed so much since you first went looking for a job that you just can't speak the language any more, and not without reason. But there's something that hasn't changed since you first started to work: employers are still interested in anything that will make life easier for them. One thing that's always in demand is a good idea. In this you're starting absolutely even with someone bursting at the seams with youth.

There's one thing to consider in this respect though. The man who built the business, who takes the responsibilities, who loves his work and will be interested in any good idea you have, sits in a corner office and you won't see him unless you make a special effort. This means getting around the personnel and employment people, who are apt to be robots who keep repeating something like, "Please fill out application form PS415." It calls for a bit of ingenuity, but it can be done. One of the best ways is to know someone who knows the owner. This is called using pull, and it's often necessary in order to pull yourself past the people out front who just want to get rid of you so that they can go on their coffee breaks. Use all the pull you can. That's not being unfair. You'll still be starting behind everyone under thirty.

Apart from salaried jobs, there are sidelines you can make extra money at. The main thing is to be realistic about it. A lot of people have sold a few paintings or handmade earrings or pottery, or they've made money raising Siamese kittens and they reason something like this: "I made ten dollars a month for the past year without even trying. When I give it my full time, if I can't make an extra thirty, forty bucks a week making those little blue pots I'll eat them." If they depend on this kind of arithmetic for food they may have to. A sideline is one thing, a business another. You may think of it as going into business just a little bit, but that little bit is subject to all vagaries of the United Steel Corporation, and you should not be too sure of the $30 or $40 a week.

A lot of people have got caught on this thing. I know one woman who found that she was rather good at making wire earrings. All her friends were in love with them and said she should make these to *sell*. She quit her job and started to make earrings for a living and suddenly found herself up to her knees in them, but she had run out of friends, and nobody else wanted them.

"If I can't sell one picture in three months, or one magazine article in three months, I'd be pretty stupid," people say. That's what you may find – that you're pretty stupid. I know I have, except that I was even more stupid because I quit a good job when I didn't have to and started writing magazine articles for a living. I left for the Mojave desert with my wife and two kids. "If I can't sell at least one article in three months I'm pretty – heh-heh – stupid," I said, and didn't sell one article in six months, although I nearly sold my wife's engagement ring to get back home.

But the thing is, a lot of the things you and your wife say when you sit with pencils poised over a clean white sheet of scratch paper, ready to mark down your rationalizations in clear, firm figures (we don't make things any more sure by pressing hard on the pencils, although we all think we do), I've done myself, years ago, and got them out of my system, whereas you still have to get them out of yours. And I've talked to other people who have done these things, and I know how these projects usually end.

A classic illustration of this sort of thing is the average man's idea of a little chicken farm in the country, or just outside some picturesque village. It has all the qualities we dream of when we're tied to salaried jobs – an independent livelihood, easy outdoor work, and a rather attractive suggestion of modest needs. One time when I lived in the country I got to know several farmers who really raised chickens and actually made money at it, and I learned a few things about this business that will keep me, for one, out of it. Most men who try to operate a nice little chicken farm end up wishing they'd never laid eyes on a chicken. They start off with some pretty exciting mathematics, with chickens multiplying geometrically all over a piece of scratch paper. Even selling at a modest sum like 50 cents a bird, they make the owner something like a couple of million dollars in four or five years. But real hens, as opposed to the ones that make money on paper, aren't nearly so obliging. They have to be fed on time or they won't lay; they tend to get slatternly and are full of troubles. They have trouble with digestion, catch cold, get cramps, and are always bordering on hysteria, and will easily panic, wiping out the owner's profits in a matter of seconds. And they work a man to death. One man can't look after more than a thousand birds and that takes him twelve to fourteen hours a day – including Sundays and holidays. If he hires someone to help, unless the owner is an experienced operator, who knows the poultry business, the hired help is the only one who shows a profit.

All this is not meant to discourage you from thinking up projects to make extra money. But when you start thinking of ways of doing it, try not to let your enthusiasm blind you to the negative possibilities. It won't hurt to go over your ideas with some cold-blooded pessimist who keeps shooting you down. You might want to jump up and down on his stomach for making discouraging remarks, but if you can hold your own with him, answer his objections, and still feel that you have a good idea, you'll be on a lot firmer ground than if you just decide it all by yourself in a euphoria of optimism.

"Getting rid of that mountain of junk...."

CHAPTER 8:
TO MOVE
OR NOT TO MOVE

Early in my life as a free-lance writer, being free to live wherever I chose, I began moving my wife and kids to places that, at the time, seemed better than the one I was in. I became generally confused by all this. I had originally decided to live in the north in the summer and in the south in the winter. But I changed my mind and moved so often that I began overlapping myself, and sometimes found myself working in Florida in summer, and arriving in Canada in mid-winter, when my hometown of Toronto looked like a scene from *Crime and Punishment*. I got Christmas cards that finally reached me in July with the message "Peace on Earth Good Will Toward Men where in hell are you living *now*?"

One time when my wife and I had checked in at the King Edward Hotel in Toronto, the girl behind the desk asked me if I'd mind telling her why I was staying at a Toronto hotel when my home was in Toronto. I didn't mind, but I couldn't for the life of me figure it out myself, and I just kept looking at my wife as if I didn't know her. All I knew was that Toronto was where I lived but I didn't live there.

I mention all this because it has given me some insight into a question faced by most people when they retire – whether to stay where they are or to retire to some place that's cheaper, quieter, sunnier or, one way or another, more desirable than the one where they've been living.

There may be some people for whom, due to a meager retirement budget, this will be a purely theoretical question. Anyone who feels that he simply can't afford to move has the decision made for him, and no harm done. There's certainly nothing wrong, or limiting, in making no major moves with retirement. The great changes in this life take place inside us, not outside us. A completely new, full, and meaningful life can be started without any alteration of living arrangements.

But I doubt if there are many people who can't afford to make a move. Except for the cost of a one-way trip, moving to another place does not necessarily involve any change in expenses; it may, and usually does, mean reduced daily living expenses. And transportation, unless it involves a move to another continent, is simply not a big economic factor. Given a car of my own that doesn't burn more than a quart of oil a hundred miles, I could move everything I need for survival, including my wife, from, say, Toronto to Florida for $75. I've done it, several times.

The great question is not an economic one, but a psychological one, and as such it involves an important decision, so important that a guide to discussions for a course in retirement, based on studies by the University of Chicago, devotes one booklet of a series to it. Their advice is to stay where you are. "If you can manage your present living arrangement financially, all the better. If you can't, and decide on a smaller place, try to stay put in a 'place of your own.' "

Some of the reasons the booklet gives for this are: "You can do things as you are used to doing them"; "You don't have to worry about 'mixing' or 'not mixing' into other people's lives"; "You can eat the types of food and follow a diet best suited for your age – without disturbing other people's"; "You (and your wife) can be masters in your own home. You can be host. Your old self-respect remains ... the grass may be greener in Florida, the climate drier in Arizona – but grass and climate cannot replace family, friends, and a community that you like and that likes you."

Lewis Mumford, an eminent observer of man in relation to his environment, and for many years architectural critic of *The New Yorker*, has much the same to say in speaking of moving to a small apartment. "This shrinkage of space is often accompanied by other losses, such as the breaking up of neighborhood ties, the abandonment of a garden and a workshop; and that in turn brings about a further contradiction of opportunities and interests ... even people in the upper income group, in robust health, may find the orbit of their lives uncomfortably narrowing...."

I can add to these arguments from my own observations and experiences. First, when you start thinking of what you could do with the money from selling your house, like buying an inexpensive little bungalow in the Caribbean or in the Rockies – one of the favourite after-dinner conversations of married couples of all ages – there are considerations that make it a good idea to put the cork back in the chianti bottle. When you try selling your house you'll find that places like yours are a drug on the market, although when you wanted one they were as scarce as love. You'll find that when strangers come in and kick your baseboards and ask you what you hope to get for the house, they'll walk away shaking their heads with sad little smiles at the greed of man. If you do sell your house, unless you sign up for another one right away, the money will tend to disappear.

There'll be certain advantages, on the other hand, if you stay in the house you already own. You won't have to worry about what to do with that mountain of stuff you've collected during most of a lifetime spent in one place. If you sell your things at auction they'll bring maybe a tenth of what they cost you and a twentieth of what they would cost if you had to buy them again; and storage will cost $30 to $40 or more a month, pending your making up your mind where you're going to live. If you do decide to ship your possessions somewhere it will cost you about what the down payment on a house used to be before the Second World War.

Another thing, there are no inexpensive little bungalows in the kind of location you're thinking of. There are $90,000 homes designed by Finnish architects to blend into the sand dunes. The inexpensive little places are on streets right out of *The Grapes of Wrath*, with rusty pickup trucks in the driveways. Maybe the street you live on now looks like that, but it doesn't to you, because you're used to it and you raised your kids there and it has so many pleasant associations that you can't see what it looks like.

A house serves as an anchor and gives stability and even a kind of respectability to your life, and without one you'll tend to drift and may get confused about where you want to live. You mightn't believe this now, looking out the window at a mixture of melted snow and soot dribbling down a brick wall, and dreaming of sunny islands and sand dunes and date palms, but being free to live wherever you want can be a major problem. I know people who, because of circumstances, suddenly found themselves free to live anywhere in the world, and have moved back and forth from places as far apart as Sydney and Toronto and Los Angeles and Montreal, absolutely incapable of deciding which end to live at, and which to visit, saying unhappily that they needed a "home base" and "headquarters" and "roots," and because they have freedom of choice, being in a state of chronic, utter indecision; one of the most painful of all states of mind.

All these are reasons why you shouldn't sell your house, and there are others. Middle-aged men and women who have left their home environment often look somehow irrelevant and out of place, like the books and things we put out on the sidewalk when we're moving. Retirement areas are full of displaced people – Winnipeg Rotarians among Florida sponge fishermen; Chicoutami lumber dealers framed in Spanish moss and banana trees; retired Hamilton Home and School presidents in communities of Salinas prune pickers; retired English doctors of philosophy in communities of Southern crackers; Georgian Bay Holstein breeders surrounded by guitars and beach bums; Bay Street brokers preparing to spend their days in communities of lobster fishermen; ex-city cops wandering Ontario villages framed in elms and looking at old Salada Tea signs, as remote from the real life of the village as Captain Bligh in the Fiji Islands, where the natives tried to eat him: retired Toronto advertising-space salesmen sitting on farm house porches amid green fields trying not to think of how little noise grass makes when it grows. The reason the silence doesn't bother the farmer is that he's involved with the land and making a living and thinking that the last time he sowed this field in peas it didn't bring in enough money to pay for his daughter's gym clothes.

But farmers can yank themselves out of context too, retiring to city apartments (so much simpler now that the kids are married and Pop has a bad back), and they're even lonelier than advertising salesmen on farms; starting compulsive conversations on the elevator about it being a bit wet under foot but by gollies we can expect it this time of year, just to hear the sound of a human voice amid those sterile mulberry-broadloomed corridors and blank cream-coloured doors; lingering in the incinerator-closet after dropping the garbage down the chute just to get a whiff of smoke from the basement furnace, which smells a little bit like an old kitchen stove.

The south is full of people who find themselves 1,500 to

3,500 miles from their homes, families, grandchildren, cronies, corner cigar stores, favourite beer parlours and barbers, and who just stand looking north, like migrating robins. I've seen men desperately start painting their houses and digging deep holes in the ground, trying to keep from thinking about the fact that they've realized their dreams.

I've been displaced. I've spent literally thousands of mornings waking up in the kind of scene people dream of on dark winter mornings. You step out the door in the morning. It's beautiful. A flotilla of pelicans soars over the dunes. The ocean makes a soothing crackling and hissing sound. Two mocking birds play tag in the Spanish bayonet. There's no one in sight. Your wife comes out of the bedroom and says she's going into town to look for a dress and just go ahead and make your own bologna sandwich for lunch. When she's gone the house begins to sound quieter. You begin listening to the ocean and the rustle of a sable palm. A mourning dove sits sobbing on a telephone wire. It's so quiet and peaceful your ears begin to feel too tight. You think nostalgically of traffic jams, crowded bars, the sound of typewriters, and the smell of carbon monoxide. It's now only nine o'clock and you have another twelve hours at least to put in. You jiggle the change in your pocket and look out at the horizon and begin wondering if something might happen to break the monotony – like an invasion from Mars. One of the really great, oversimplified, wrong ideas of man is that being happy is just a matter of moving into a beautiful scene.

But there's another side to all this. I sold my house once and went to Greece and it was great. That year my wife and I were probably the only people in Europe who had sold their house to get there. I had no regrets. Just listening to Athens wake up in the morning was worth it.

Getting rid of that mountain of junk most of us collect when we live for thirty-five or forty years in one place isn't necessarily a bad idea, even if we have to sell it for next to nothing. We can get too bogged down with things – tools, books, chinaware, keepsakes, knicknacks, snapshots, old pants that are still too good to throw out even if zoot suits are a bit out of style. We can fool ourselves about holding on to these things "for the kids." I know people who are holding on to old homesteads for "kids" who will never want them except to sell them and go to Spain. Or people who are holding onto summer cottages for the kids, four-foot-sets of Dickens for the kids, and canoes for the kids, and silver tea pots for the kids and mattresses and overcoats and watchmaker's tools for the kids. It's a mistake. By and large nobody wants these things.

There's a lot of guff written, too, about the horrors of taking your chances with a new way of life. "What would you do if you got sick or something, away from home among strangers?"

I have been sick or something among strangers, and I've been given a hand so often by people I've never seen before in my life that I've sometimes wondered if we don't behave better toward one another as strangers than we do as friends. Most of us spend our lives behind a set of defences, guarding our jobs, prejudices, money, dignity, self-respect, lawns, and egos. But as strangers we can drop our defences. We know the other guy isn't a threat. He's just another human, standing on a street corner or beside a stalled car with a confused look. Our impulse is to help him. It's when we know him, and have time to think things over and wonder what he ever did for us, that we get cautious about behaving like Christians.

Only you know how you'll feel about change and travel and starting a new way of life. Only you know whether you get homesick. I know I do. I get homesick for Canada whenever I leave it for too long, and, something that will strike many Canadians as incomprehensible, I get homesick for Toronto. People in Vancouver will flatly refuse to believe this, but it's true.

Yet nomadic traits appear in surprising places. I've known

middle-aged people who seemed as set in their ways as if they'd been dropped in cement, who suddenly pulled up stakes, sold everything but a piece of Blue Mountain pottery, a hooked rug that was given to them by an aunt in Moonstone, and moved into a pink concrete-block efficiency in Fort Myers, Scotch-taped some supermarket art to the wall, and by evening were settled into their new life as comfortably as if they'd dug in beside the Mill on the Floss.

One man I know, a retired department store executive, outwardly the soul of permanence, conservatism, and dignity, gets a certain amount of pleasure from telling people, when they ask him where he's living now, "In a trailer." He divides his time between a trailer in Florida and a cottage in Muskoka. I've seen the trailer park where he stays and it's one of the few I've ever seen that I would live in.

Most trailer parks have all the charm of a used-car lot. Housetrailers, by the way, are now called mobile homes, although they're not very mobile any more. They're pulled from place to place by those tractors with "wide load" on the bumper, but not many people move them. People buy and sell them without moving them, like houses. They're surprisingly roomy when you get inside them – with panelled living rooms, breakfast nooks, modern kitchens, bathtubs, bars. Two people can rattle around in one of these things and go away and leave it and it will be looked after on a special deal with the trailer park people for something like $5 a month.

Something to keep in mind, if you're considering a life of migrating from south or north semi-annually: Canadian crown lands are sold or leased in most provinces, most of it in areas too rugged for cultivation but just right for people who like to wake up in the morning listening to chickadees and Whiskey Jacks and watching the mist lift off Canada's lakes and hard-rock forests. The lots are usually available far below the prices asked by private sellers, and the requirements are modest – the construction of a cottage within a year or two, costing around $2,500. But don't make the mistake of thinking of these places to "homestead," an expression that went out with the Great Depression. They are for summer cottages only.

But whether you live in a trailer or cottage, or move to another home in another part of the world, the final decision, whether to stay put or pull up stakes, is a personal one, dependent on the very inner workings of your own nature. There are no rules in making a decision except to try to see things in terms of what you really know about yourself, rather than in hackneyed formulas, like "there's no place like home," or "travel broadens the mind." We all have a tendency to mental laziness in this regard – to get just one idea and hang onto it without ever really examining it. A sports writer I know tells a story I always liked about being shipped off to boarding school as a kid. For a year and a half he resented it, complained about it bitterly, until, without realizing it, he was rather enjoying listening to himself complain. Then one day, right in the middle of cursing his parents and the school and his bad luck, the thought came to him, clear and cool, out of nowhere – "I *like* this school."

That's the kind of truth to strive for in deciding whether you're going to move or not.

"He made a vow that if God spared him and he got home he would never leave the desert again. . . ."

CHAPTER 9: RETIREMENT IN AND OUT OF CANADA

My wife and I once started studying maps of humidity and precipitation and mean annual temperatures, determined to choose, on a calm, scientific basis, the ideal place to live, and finally, by sheer logic, decided on a little white spot about the size of a pea on a map of Arizona. We ended up at 5,000 feet above sea level in a deserted ski resort talking to the family of a rather lonely fish and wildlife man. We hadn't taken altitude into our calculations, or mankind, for that matter, and we'd overlooked the fact that precipitation can be all snow.

Choosing a perfect place to retire is not a science; it's more like falling in or out of love – it's all done with the senses. Weather statistics tell you everything about the weather except the one thing you want to know – what's it like? Real estate prices can, and usually do, leave out things like adjoining insul-brick shacks and old car bodies – in other words, one of the most important, if not the most important, factor – – the feeling of the place.

Subject to these very important qualifications, the following places are suggested for consideration, because of one reason or another – the restful pace of daily life, the low living expenses, the beautiful scenery, the sunshine, the moderate or snowless winters. But anyone contemplating moving to any of them should, if at all possible, make at least one and preferably two or three visits there first, and should stay long enough each time to get over the novelty and begin to know something of the people, the economics, and the year-round climate.

The Maritimes is a region of bagpipes, beautiful scenery, fishing villages, forests, the sea, and a relatively sane and civilized pace of life, or, as one young enthusiast for her native province of Nova Scotia put it: "People go to bed early, get up early, and don't live in apartments."

The weather, in most tourist material, ends with Indian summer, which everyone agrees is beautiful, but winter is bypassed. Still, the winters are tempered by the sea, and in the Annapolis valley the snowfall is light. Cape Breton, which is cross-hatched by inlets and sounds, has beaches facing every direction. Retirees from inland Canada love to live near the sea and drive to places like Peggy's Cove and explore the islands. You could spend the rest of your life just exploring the Canadian history that has taken place in this region.

Halifax is a community that has preserved some of the best features of city life without picking up a lot of the bad ones. Bridgetown, in the Annapolis Valley, is becoming the centre of a retirement area.

Fredericton, New Brunswick, is a prim, tidy place, very gung-ho British. Saint John, at the mouth of the St. John River, is a hilly old port built on solid rock with weathered old gray, green, and buff clapboard houses perched on steep streets, some of them overlooking, to the north, the distant blue mountains that recede, fold upon fold into the mist. New Brunswick is a fisherman's paradise. The Miramichi and the Restigouche are among the world's most famous salmon streams. There are often as many millionaires on the wilds of the Restigouche as there are on Bay Street.

Prince Edward Island is reached by ferry and some people may feel cut off there, but it's a well-known fact that Prince Edward Islanders feel that it's the rest of Canada that's cut off from *them*. You can drive across the province in twenty-five minutes. It's full of friendly, chatty people; it's untouched by big-city traffic, smog, billboards, suburban sprawl, or bad manners. Sociologically, the province is one big small town made up of 108,000 neighbours, with miles of vegetable gardens in between. It's one of the most beautiful provinces, and literally the most colourful – dark-green potato fields, ice-green oats, emerald-green grass, dark-green spruce and balsam making patterns against the spectacular red of the island's soil. Highway shoulders are red, Rocks are red. Cliffs are red. Beaches are red. Kids, playing in the dirt, get as red as freshly-dug Prince Edward Island potatoes.

Victoria, the capital of British Columbia, on Juan de Fuca Straight at the south end of Vancouver Island is the most popular retirement spot in Canada. Between 600 and 700 people go there yearly, about half of them British-born. It's balmy, with golf and flowers in mid-winter, almost surrounded by the sea, something like the best resorts on the south coast of Britain. It's generally sunny, seldom snows, and then not much. Rents are high, and places sometimes hard to find, but it's clean and quiet, the scenery is magnificent, with a view of the ocean and mountains, swans in the parks, ships in the harbour from Hawaii, New Zealand, California, Australia; sight-seeing trips to the forests and waterfalls at Vancouver Island.

"What do I like about Victoria? Everything," an Ottawa woman, quoted in an article on Victoria by Geronimo Vie in *Weekend Magazine*, said. "Just two days in Victoria and

I had made up my mind to live here. The weather was gorgeous, even though it was mid-winter. The daffodils were in full bloom ... the sea, the mountains with snow on them ... everything just ideal. It was what I wanted. I had thought I could get all this only in England. Even the shops, particularly the shops in Bastion Square ... I can't believe you can have this all in one city."

BELOW THE SNOWLINE

To many Canadians retirement means retirement from snow, and it has given rise to a kind of Canadian backlash – the conviction that there's a monotony about sub-tropical latitudes that has a deadly effect on the spirit, while frost has an ennobling and invigorating influence and produces superior characters. George Orwell long ago pointed out that the English, who also hold this belief, never carry it to the point of claiming that Eskimos are therefore infinitely superior to Englishmen.

Although it's true that the change of seasons is not the same as in the north, there *are* seasons, different in mood and feeling and climate. The Atlantic Ocean in the winter gets black and white instead of the pale, milky green of summer; the spindrift shivers on the beaches and gulls stand facing northeast to keep from getting blown away. In the spring, in Florida, for instance, there's a delicate green veil of leaves on the dead-looking cypresses. The California and Arizona deserts bloom.

"I wouldn't feel it was Christmas without snow" is a common remark that doesn't make much sense. There's nothing un-Christmaslike about what southerners call a pretty day, when the salt spray glistens in the air like crystals and the palms sparkle in the morning sun and the big translucent leaves of the banana trees shine like Christmas displays.

Christmas is very Christmassy in the south, with religious pageants under the moon and a holy light on the palm trees – without the distraught shoppers and desperate drinkers, downtown slush, stalled buses, frustrated pedestrians. It's true that department-store Santa Clauses are often sad-looking, lean Southern crackers, but then Santa Claus up north when you get up close to him is pretty awful too.

I'm not suggesting that everyone, or anyone, should retire below the snowline. I like snow myself, and – something I find hard to make convincing to most people, including my wife – I actually like feeling cold. But anyone who does want to move south shouldn't worry too much about missing the seasons. He won't miss the seasons if he has any sensitivity to the changes of nature. And there's no question about it, life in a snow-free climate is easier and simpler than it is up north. When you go outside the house, you just go out. You don't put on any different clothes than you were wearing lying on the couch. Below the snowline, the automobile – probably the greatest single contribution to human agony in winter – remains a convenience all year. You never have to dig it out, defrost the windshield, thaw the rad, drive it on ice, leave it stuck in a drift, or nearly die of cold trying to get it started.

Florida is visited by about 75,000 Canadians a year, many with a chip on their shoulders, ready to compare it with the Rockies (it's not as high). Many decide to retire there permanently. It's a sub-tropical land of swamp, mildew, Spanish moss, live oaks, prickly plants, savannas, beaches, pine woods, lagoons and palms; sometimes shacky, often beautiful, always accommodating, because much of it is resort area. Living is inexpensive, in housekeeping flats, in bleached clapboard private houses on the beach of inland, or in "efficiencies," like motel rooms with baths and kitchens.

Most winter days the sun is as warm as the sun in, say,

Montreal in July. But cold spells can bring the temperature down to frost level at night, and into the fifties in the daytime, about like good Canadian football weather, but too cold for sunbathing, and very disappointing for people who come down for two weeks' holidays and who conclude that Florida is a hoax. These cold spells come in December to February, usually last a couple of days, then the weather warms up again to the average kind of day described above.

There's always a lot of power in the sun. If your feet are cold and you stand in a patch of sun on the living-room rug, it's like putting them up to an electric heater. In spring and fall the weather is hot: in summer in the high nineties, but you never feel stifled. Humidity softens the air. Although if you try working indoors, you start to dissolve, and if you sit in the shade in the ocean breeze you get chilly. Most tormenting thing is the invasion, at sun-up and sun-down, of sand flies. They have an incredible charge of itching, swelling juice, they love young Canadians in bikinis, fresh from being snowed on, and will raise welts the size of quarters.

Late summer and fall is hurricane time. I went through Donna and enjoyed it, but it only wound up to 120 miles an hour, just enough to be dramatic. The reports over the radio put it closer and closer till someone said, "The eye is over Samsula," and then everything went dead, and we knew The Thing was right out there in our back yard pounding our house with big fists, while we huddled around lamps made of Nescafe jars and candles.

Coastal California is an entirely different thing. There's rarely a feeling of tremendous heat, and it's so free of bugs you don't need screens. The beach towns smell of suntan lotion, kelp, the sea, wet rocks, salt, mist, and broiled steaks, and they are unquestionably among the most beautiful places in the world. Whether you would like the area or not is something else. To many, it seems self-conscious, contrived, artificial, full of uprooted people. My wife one time pointed to a house and asked a real estate woman if it was for sale. The woman replied, "Every house is for sale. What we're concerned about is the price." Don't make the mistake of lumping southern and northern California together. People in San Francisco feel as remote from southern Californians as British Columbians do from the people of San Francisco.

The Desert, covers all Arizona, Nevada, and most of California. Some people hate it, some love it. It's perpetually sunny, although it can get frosty on winter mornings; and the desert air is so clear you constantly miscalculate distances. In summer it's like a brick kilne, and so dry it will make picnic sandwiches feel like toast five minutes after they've been taken from the Glad Bags.

People who were born and raised in the desert can't understand why everybody doesn't live there. I talked to one man – an old railway man who had been in the First World War – and he told me that he sat in a tent in France one time after it had rained for a month, looking at the mould on his shoes and the puddles outside the tent and thinking of the desert. He made a vow that if God spared him and he got home he would never leave the desert again and he never did. An odd thing about the desert: although it's beautiful, lonely, and majestic, the towns men build there are barren, mean, ugly, and depressing – to me anyway.

Whether the desert is good for various afflictions, like arthritis, is something I wouldn't dream of having an opinion on. I can't see how it could be bad for it, but there's a whole kind of medical mythology about people who came down there in shawls and wheelchairs and within a few months of being baked in the sun were trotting around like Joe Namath. I do know there's big difference between the heat in the desert and the heat, say, in a Toronto apartment in July. I remember carrying one of my children on my shoulders for two miles coming home from a local fair. I arrived home not the least bit tired to discover that the temperature was 102 in the shade, and that my front door knob was so hot I had to wrap a fist-full of my jacket around it before I could open the door. If you like that kind of heat, and if it makes you feel better, a desert town like Needles, California, is the place to get it.

San Franciso, a snow-free but sometimes foggy and rainy place, comes closer to a Mediterranean city than any other place in North America, with glimpses of blue sea, streets of close-packed cream or white plaster-faced buildings coming right to the sidewalk, the whole city flowing over hills and as sharply lit in the sunlight as a stage set. There are vast areas of wooden clapboard Victorian buildings that have been there since 1906 and look as if they'll be there until 2006, complete with carved masks, peaks, shields, cones, spires, dormers, bow windows, cupids, knobs, and turrets.

Old-time San Franciscans consider the view from a room or apartment very important, and a landlord will lead you past coffee-stained rugs, broken bedsteads, and a stove with knobs missing to point out a view of Golden Gate bridge or of a flower garden a hundred feet below. Roof-sitting there is a custom so simple and uncomplicated that only an old, sophisticated city would think of it. Most San Francisco apartments have some kind of arrangement, maybe just a sheet metal deck or a patch of gravel enclosed by a peeling picket fence, where you can – well, sit on the roof – in a thicket of TV aerials and laundry lines, amid the smell of bacon and eggs, mist, wet gravel, peeling paint and hot rust, with San Francisco Bay gleaming in the east like a sheet of old silver, and green hills to the south and behind them distant mountains the colour of faded blue jeans. Sometimes morning fog covers patches of the city and the sunlit tops of tall buildings protrude from it like some other city in the sky, and there's just the song of a California housefinch and, in the background, like a bass fiddle, a distant fog horn giving an anguished moan, with a sudden drop at the end, as if somebody knocked the breath out of it.

San Francisco is surrounded by the sea. You're always looking over the city as if you were coming in for a landing. You look down on ships so far off you'd think they were standing still if it weren't for the white water at their bows. Buses, even a short distance away, appear to be climbing vertical walls. Cabs suddenly appear at intersections as if they were coming out of deep ditches.

My last recollection of San Francisco is of sitting in Union Square downtown on a drowsy day watching a tall angry looking man with a sandwich board walking around stirring up the pigeons and shouting, "Eat no pork or fat or blood. Drink no tea. Jesus will soon be here, and he doesn't like women with short hair or men with long hair."

He never looked at the people, who rarely looked at him. Once a roustabout in blue jeans, clutching a battered guitar in one hand, roused himself from the grass, yelled, "You tell 'em, Pop," and fell back, collapsing with the effort, flinging an arm over his eyes.

"You never saw a baby born with earrings," the tall man snapped over his shoulder. "A lot of people are going to hell. Men with long hair will never get to heaven."

Every now and then hundreds of pigeons swept over the park about eight feet above the heads of the crowd, casing it for chocolate-bar chips, with a sound like a great fan starting up.

"Britain is the backbone of civilization," a patriarch with long white eyebrows yelled. The pigeons swept back again. Everybody dozed.

The West Indies, a 2,500 mile archipelago of thousands of islands curving from the vicinity of Florida to South America, is divided into three main groups – The Bahama Islands, the Greater Antilles (Cuba, Jamaica, Hispaniola and Puerto Rico), and the Lesser Antilles (the Leeward Islands, Windward Islands, Trinidad, Barbados, and the Dutch and Venezuelan Islands).

The Caribbean is never oppressively hot; the warmer islands are the farthest south, but they're tempered by the trade winds, and in the upper Bahamas the winters can be downright chilly. Temperatures vary with altitude and with distance from the shore. Generally the islands are warm and sunny and breezy with only slightly higher temperatures in summer. In most islands, the cost of living is a lot lower than in Canada. There are no fuel bills, no heavy clothing to buy. You can have a vegetable garden year round.

Some parts of the West Indies are touristy and crowded (particularly in the winter season) but there are many quiet islands – places like Montserrat in the British Leeward Islands and St. Lucia and Saint Vincent in the Windward Islands. Medical services are adequate, but in many places may not be as plentiful as in Canada and are more likely to be concentrated in one well-equipped hospital. But before deciding to move to the West Indies, go there on a visit, read about them, and look into the social and political background of the particular island you're interested in.

Mexico. There's lots of desert in Mexico. Driving through some places, like Baja California, is like driving over the moon. But there are also mountains and steaming tropical jungles. The climate varies with the altitude, so that although the country lies mostly in the tropics, there are regions of hot, temperate, and cool lands. An immigrant to Mexico has to have the usual police clearance and prove he has an adequate income, from outside the country, of around $250 a month for himself plus about $85 a month for each dependent over fifteen years old, and he has to prove he can meet these conditions for a minimum of five years. Foreigners can buy property, on the same basis as Mexicans, with two exceptions (1) in certain cases they have to sign a waver of the right of diplomatic intervention, and (2) there are certain properties they can't obtain, for reasons of national defence; for instance, they can't *own* land within thirty miles of the sea or sixty miles of an international border.

Europe. The low-priced, sunny areas, by and large, are in Spain, Greece, and Portugal. Spain is one of the cheapest countries in the world to live in. Ibiza, in the Balearic Islands in the Mediterranean off Spain, currently a popular spot, is gradually raising its prices, but is still inexpensive. In places like Torremolinos, and Malaga, a fifteen-cent tip still gets a salute.

In Portugal, moderately-priced areas are Cascais and Estoril outside Lisbon, on the Atlantic, and Lisbon itself, an old and charming city where a room in a good hotel for a week, with breakfast, costs about what a Toronto or Montreal hotel or a Holiday Inn charges for a room for one night.

Greece is one of the cheapest of all places. The weather is superb – deep-blue skies and constant sunshine. The Aegean is dotted with islands and with primitive picturesque villages where the Canadian dollar goes a long way. In Athens, a spare but clean and comfortable room with private bath and a balcony overlooking Omonia (Harmony) Square, a main hub of action in the non-tourist part of town, costs three or four dollars a night for two. Basic fare in taxis is 15 cents. You can get a drink of ouzo for 10 cents, a bottle of wine for 43 cents, a quarter of a baked chicken with mashed potatoes for about 60 cents. A couple can have dinner out and a movie for $2.00. Trips are very inexpensive. A two-hour bus ride from Athens to Sunium, on the far southeast coast of Attica, a town that was in the news about 2,000 years before Columbus reached America, and the site of the shrine of Poseidon, one of the most spectacular sights in Greece, costs $1.36, return.

Most of these places have tourist bureaus in major Canadian cities, and consulates where you can get all the details about immigration requirements. The main concern is whether you have enough money to support yourself. Having established that, it's a matter of getting a visa, and there are usually short-stay and long-stay visas, which involve having your picture taken, getting a police statement that you have no criminal record, getting a passport and vaccination certificate, all of which are routine and usually cost very little.

One of the advantages of staying in Canada is that you avoid all this kind of red-tape. British Columbia, Nova Scotia, New Brunswick, and Prince Edward Island are, at time of writing, still part of Canada, and you don't need any papers to go there. For the United States, up to six months you don't need any either. If you're going to stay, you require a U.S. Immigration visa, which permits you to live and work there and do most things except vote or run for president. This is not "taking out papers" as it used to be called. You are as Canadian as you always were. You just happen to be living in the United States.

But don't apply for a visa unless you're pretty sure it's going to be a permanent move as it just complicates things. You can't live in two places; you can have only one legal address. It can be a back bedroom in Moosejaw and you don't ever need to be there, but you have to name one place as your permanent address and stick to it, or people like the folks down at the Motor Vehicle Branch of the Department of Transport will hate you, and so will your bank manager, the Department of Internal Revenue, and the subscription departments of magazines.

The process of getting a U.S. visa ends with you having a little green plastic card about the size of your oil-company credit card. It's called a border-crossing card and works fine at the border, but thousands of Canadians, after getting these cards, have changed their minds about living in the States. At the same time they figure there's no point in giving up the card voluntarily, after all that trouble of getting it, so they just keep the card and live in Canada. This is what I did. I'd had one U.S. visa, then had given it up. Then I changed my mind and got another visa, then began living in Canada again most of the time, but this time I just held on to my U.S. visa. When I came to Toronto I came as a Canadian citizen permanently residing in the United States who was visiting his home in Canada – I think. It all came to an end one sunny morning at the Peace Bridge, where I arrived, in the process of a rather complicated move, with so many odds and ends in the car I couldn't have looked more suspicious if I'd had a loose hand on the seat beside me. I got into a strange dialogue with a short, swarthy immigration man with lively, suspicious eyes and no neck.

"What have you got there in that bag?"

"What bag?"

"That bag on the back seat."

"I'll just take a look."

"Why do you have to look to know what you've got in a bag? Just tell me what's in it."

"I don't *know* what's in it."

"Is this your car?"

"Yes – I think so."

"Just pull over to the side there."

I've often tried to reconstruct the sequence of questions and answers that took place that morning. I remember coming apart and volunteering information, like the fact that my TV didn't work very well, when nobody had even asked me if I had one, only to discover I was now technically smuggling American-made TV's into the United States which somehow, I'll never know how, lead to somebody asking me where I paid my taxes. By now I looked as if I paid them to the Kremlin, and the immigration officer lifted my visa and told me congenially, while he was typing out the forms, that he'd always wanted to be a writer himself.

"I've seen places near the ocean that would take Ponce de Leon a week to reach with dug-out canoes."

CHAPTER 10:
FOR YOUR PROTECTION

An important thing to keep in mind is that the retired market is now a big and juicy one. Retired people are prime targets for crooks and near crooks and promoters, and often are self-victims of a kind of financial euphoria that sometimes accompanies retirement. All this takes place when it can least be afforded. A book entitled *You, the Law and Retirement* by Virginia Lehmann, put out by the U.S. Department of Health, Education and Welfare, points out that when you retire "your margin for error begins to disappear, so it is important to avoid mistakes if you can. As a young working man or woman you could recoup your losses if you made a mistake. Now you may not have a chance to do so."

Anyone approaching retirement should keep a sharp eye on the legal aspect of his affairs. He should have a legal check-up regularly, just as he has a physical one, and a new legal check-up whenever there is any major change in circumstances: a death in the family, or a birth, a marriage, divorce, or, the above booklet says, a "change in your financial condition whether for better or worse." This is particularly important if you're moving from one part of the country to another, or from one country to another, because laws change from place to place.

The best time to line up a lawyer is when things are calm and normal, instead of at a time when it's necessary to grab one in an emergency, and it's easy to pick a shyster. You can get the name of a good lawyer from a friend or by phoning the local bar association or city hall, and when you do get a lawyer, ask him how much he charges, or, at any rate, get some idea of what it's going to cost you, which he'll be glad to tell you if he isn't getting ready to scalp you. The help of a lawyer is very important if you're making out a will or starting a business; especially if you're using your home for a business. He can also help you find out about what benefits you have coming and what you should do about collecting them, long before you retire. Even the government can't start paying you unless you give them some idea that you're retiring.

Everyone needs a lawyer when buying or selling a house, or buying a co-operative or condominium apartment and it's not a bad idea to have one when making arrangements with your children, such as turning over the house to them on the understanding that they'll look after you. It should be a straightforward business deal or you may be sorry. Although parents and children are sometimes shy of talking over financial details, it's been the experience of lawyers that they don't stay shy for long.

Prepare for a barrage of promotional literature inviting you to do everything from joining lonely hearts clubs and writing courses to fitting yourself with false teeth. One government pamphlet putting the elderly and lonely on their guard says solemnly, "You can't buy love," and I can tell you you can't buy the ability to write – you work for it, with your hair in your eyes, by yourself. Writing courses are useless. This doesn't mean, by the way, that they're crooked. Most teachers in writing courses really think you can teach people to write. But in twenty-five years I've known only one writer who can really write and who took a writing course, and even he doesn't recommend it. The only person I've ever known who got anything out of a class in writing was a divorcee who got the teacher, a friend of mine, an old pro who did his best to teach people how to write short stories, without success. But getting a writer for a husband is not much of a graduation present.

When you go on motor trips don't believe anything a service-station operator tells you. He may be honest, but on the road you have no way of knowing, and there are plenty who wait for grey-haired gents and their wives 2,500 miles from home to try to scare the whey out of them by telling them their fuel pumps are leaking, their shock absorbers are going to buckle, their coil housing cracking. I've had all these things and more told to me within the past year, but I haven't changed the coils, shocks, rad or fuel pump and the car is running just fine. (Unfortunately, I began believing nothing a service station man said. So when one shifty-looking man told me my fan belt was ready to go I ignored him, and it fell off the next day.)

If you're on a motor trip don't leave your car temptingly displayed with your camera and binoculars and a package of Canadian tea on view in the rear window advertising that you're touring and that your car is loaded. Locking it doesn't mean anything. Thieves can get your ventilator windows open with a coat hanger faster than you can turn around, and from there on it's easy. The trunk is the safest spot. I once had $600 worth of things (my wife and I had just given up an apartment on one of our many moves and had enough stuff in the car to set up housekeeping again) cleaned out of my car in San Francisco. The trunk wasn't touched but the only things they left inside the car were my wife's Vogue patterns and our books, although, oddly, they stole the complete works of Aristotle.

Don't ever go into any schemes that involve your buying

or renting equipment without checking with a lawyer, or you may end up with just the machine and a hole in your savings account, along with the one in your head.

Here are some of the most common fakes and swindles. A machine that costs $875 and supposedly tells you what's wrong with you (if you'd pay $875 for it there's plenty). Air Purifiers for preventing or treating colds, some of which are touted as "Negative Generators." Cures for alcoholism, arthritis, baldness, or impotence. Don't buy any wonder gloves with uranium-ore linings, electro-magnetic bracelets, mail-order false teeth or eyeglasses, bottled sea water, wrinkle removers, or anything that will reverse the death process into the life process for $30 (or $3); tonics that slow down the aging process by supplying as much essential iron as forty pints of raw oysters, nine pounds of beefsteak, ninety-three pounds of spinach, or sixty pounds of fish; any cure that hinges on your standing naked in a dark room with your hands pointing north. Don't buy Stagg Bullets or Genuine Passionaola, a preparation for women which contains sugar, the juice of pineapple, papaya, peach, apricot, apple, grape, and passion fruit. Don't believe anything an astrologer, crystal-ball reader, or tarot-card reader tells you; just put it down to a couple of bucks worth of fun, like shooting crap. Don't believe anyone who says you've been selected for something because you're such a distinguished character. Don't talk to anyone who tries to sell you anything over the phone.

One of the rackets that took place a few months ago in a small town I go to in Florida hinges on people being good public-minded citizens. (There's always a flurry of rackets in the fall when the grifters are going to Miami, and in the spring, when they're coming back). Just three days after a repeat TV program on *Dragnet* exposed a bank-examiner racket, an elderly woman was taken in by the same racket run by some guy who never left a telephone booth opposite a Winn Dixie Supermarket. He phoned her and told her that he was an auditor at the local bank where she had her savings account. ("How did he know I had $1,800 in my account?" she asked a detective later. "You told him," the detective reminded her. All the man had said was that she had an account at the bank of so-and-so, and she had said, "Yes. I have $1,800.")

Funds, the man said, had been disappearing from savings accounts and she was to go to the bank (the caller would have her picked up and taken there by cab) and draw out $1,500 in small bills, which would later be marked to catch the crooked teller, and take the cab home.

The woman obediently took the cab, and drew out the money. When she got home, she'd just come in the front door when the phone rang and the same voice told her a man would be there in a few minutes to pick up the money. He was there in three minutes, she handed him the money and he handed her an envelope, tipped his hat, and left.

One group operating in the same area gathers up oil from service stations, picks up a couple of shingles at some construction site, and goes around with the story that they have just finished a roofing job for Mrs. So-and-so down the street and had some very expensive shingles and cement left over and they'll do that front porch in an hour for $29.50, payable in advance. Then they disappear with the oil and shingles.

So many "little old ladies" are victims of these people that it creates a false confidence that it can't happen to little young ladies or big old men, but it does. Most people who retire seem to take a peculiar switch about looking after their affairs. All bankers know this. One of the things that amaze bankers below the snowbelt is that hard-headed businessmen from the north, men who have been running factories and sales organizations and their own businesses, come down to retirement areas acting as if they left their brains up north with their galoshes. One banker told me, "I had a man in here yesterday, a retired tool-and-die manufacturer from

Montreal. He came down here last week, saw a house at night in the rain, and signed up to buy it. Then he found it was 400 feet from a bar and next door to a guy who raised dogs, and the next day he tried to get out of it." Up until his retirement this man would have fired anyone in his staff who bought anything with no more thought than that. But after a lifetime dream of a little bungalow in the sun, suddenly seeing it there, real and solid, even if it was in the rain, dripping beneath the palmettos, the businessman in him went bonkers. Some men, when they retire, suddenly let their wives handle all business matters after a lifetime of keeping them in the dark about any expenditure bigger than the price of a pot roast.

I know one retired man who went for a drive one Sunday morning and before he came back had bought a house he didn't want, in a town he didn't like, for a price he couldn't afford. He had slowed down opposite a house for sale, and a young real estate agent had come out and said he could show him a better house for sale. The man followed him as if under some kind of hypnosis, and within an hour had signed all the forms. Looking back the closest he could come to explaining it was that he always liked black brogues, which he noticed the salesman was wearing. He couldn't believe anyone who wore black brogues could be dishonest. In this case, at any rate, he was right. The salesman, who could have nailed him, let him out of the deal and returned his deposit.

Don't ever buy property without seeing it. The claims may be, and probably are, literally true. In Florida, for instance, when they say "near the ocean," they're probably telling the truth. I've seen places near the ocean that would take Ponce de Leon a week to reach with dug-out canoes. The ocean has a habit of ending in instalments of lagoons, swamps, dunes, savannas, everglades, inland waterways, and mangrove swamps. One man I know has got used to Northerners ringing his bell and asking him where 285 Palmetto Boulevard is.

"It's right near the ocean," they say. "I own a lot there. I bought it up north." He takes them up to his sun deck and points. "It should be right about over there," he says, pointing to a jungle of cabbage palms, palmetto scrub, Spanish bayonette, sandspurs, bamboo, cactus, and swamp. "Oh, no, that's not it," the caller says, getting sore. "This place they already had the bulldozers in there and some of the sidewalks down."

But, as a matter of fact, although everyone should be on guard against crooks, and semi-crooks, and unconscious crooks and people who remain honest by an arrangement of mirrors, the ones to watch the closest are the ones who are absolutely legal – the promoters who imply, or state flatly, that happiness is a matter of swimming pools, sun, boats, golf courses, and not having to work. Florida promotion literature, with pictures of women standing in front of sloops falling apart with sex, never sticks at making flat statements about how to be happy. "Did you know that over 25,000 retirees already live happily in the Daytona Beach, Florida, resort area?" one says. "Happiness is living in Award-Winning Briarwood Mobile Estates." "A Paradise Awaits You in Clermont." Realism plays no place in the minds of the people who write these things. "Loafing can be hard if you have never done it before. But Englewoods' sunny climate makes loafing easy and fun."

Selling the old dream of Shangri-La is really a more dangerous one than selling you shock absorbers you don't need. I've taken illustrations from Florida because a lot of Canadians go there when they retire, not because there are any more con-artists there than anywhere else. Canada has its full quota. I like Florida, and I like a lot of the places that are promoted for the wrong reasons. I'm just pointing out that taking a good long, hard look at these things is part of the process of preparing for retirement.

"This proposal looks interesting. . . . Watch Myrtle while I read it over."

CHAPTER II: HEALTH

From desk-bound accountants with postures like pelicans, to salesmen slumped in Buicks with their belt buckles scraping the steering wheels, most people, by the time they reach retirement, are pot-bellied, round-shouldered, and short of wind, with no more muscular tone than an old mattress. Most of us look as if we're kidding in shorts, either pulling them under our armpits or letting them droop, with the waistband concealed beneath a paunch that has an overhang like a thatched cottage.

A barrage of booklets, magazine articles, mimeographed bulletins, films and speeches by those who make a study of retirement, all stress the importance, when retirement comes, of organizing a schedule of walking, exercise, golf, swimming, dieting – whatever it takes to get into physical shape, to build up muscle tone, and to get rid of excess fat, which is a threat to health. J.G. Clarkson, Medical Director, Department of Public Health, Saskatchewan, says: "Nearly all major illnesses in later years are adversely affected by being overweight." An excess of food is stored as fat under the skin and around internal organs. Each extra pound of body fat requires about a quarter of a mile of blood vessels, which makes a lot of extra work for the heart. "The need for food essentially depends on how active you are and as you grow older you tend to be less active and so require slightly less food," says Doctor Clarkson. "However, it is important to see that your diet is properly balanced, and essential factors that must be maintained in your diet are proteins, minerals, and vitamins. Put in plain language, your diet has to contain sufficient meat, fish, milk, eggs, cheese, green and yellow vegatables and fruit to supply these needs."

Anyone living alone has to be on guard against making do with inadequate meals, Doctor Clarkson says, or missing them altogether, just because cooking becomes too much bother. "Much can be done to guard against carelessness in food habits by making a point of going out for the odd meal and by entertaining your friends. If you live by yourself you might decide to take turns in preparing and sharing meals with others and company is an excellent stimulus to the appetite."

The chief difference between the diet for the earlier and later adult years is the amount of energy food needed. Older people need less food solely for energy. They are usually less active and their body processes have slowed down.

Quality of food rather than quanity should be stressed. Emphasis should be on protein, minerals, and vitamins, rather than fats and sugars. The latter provide calories only – they're lacking on other things the body needs.

A reliable guide is put out by the Nutrition Division of the Department of National Health and Welfare – *Good Eating with Canada's Food Guide.* This is to the point, with enough detail to let you know why you need various foods. It gives a daily plan involving five categories of food, which supply all the nutrients your body needs: protein for growth and repair; fats and carbohydrates for energy, vitamins and minerals for efficient body functions. Most local municipal health departments have it, and if not you can get it by writing the Nutrition Divison, Department of Health and Welfare in Ottawa. A more complete publication – *Healthful Eating*, is available for 50 cents from the Queen's Printer book stores.

By following a well-balanced diet you avoid food that will put on weight, which is hard on your heart. Another way to ease the burden on your heart is to exercise. It's a well-documented fact that the less active the life, the harder the heart has to work. Although the heart is a very efficient machine – 100 per cent more efficient in fuel-energy ratio than an automobile – it loses efficiency without exercise. For example, the heart beat of a person in good shape from exercise is around 85 beats a minute while climbing a flight of stairs; for a person who doesn't get enough exercise, it's 155. One study showed that a person who had ridden a stationary bike twenty minutes a day, four days a week, for eighty-four days, had a heart beat of 140 beats a minute compared to one hundred-and seventy before the first ride on the first day.

A book called *Good Health, Personal and Community*, by Benjamin F. Miller and John J. Burt, shows the electrocardiograms of an eighty-seven-year-old mountain climber with a heart beat of forty-eight a minute, and sixty-nine-year-old woman who, for some unexplained reason, stayed in bed voluntarily for thirty years, who had a heart rate of one hundred-and-forty. The same book points out that a tame rabbit has a heart rate of approximately two-hundred beats a minute, whereas the wild hare has a rate of around sixty-four beats a minute. It has been computed that for sedentary office workers the daily work load of the heart, measured in units called killogram meters, is between 10,000 to 15,000; for athletes, 5,000 to 10,000, with an oxygen consumption of 25 to 40 cubic centimeters a minute for the sedentary group as compared to 15 to 25 cubic centimeters a minute for the athletes.

There are all kinds of books of exercises on the market. One of the most popular, which you might enjoy, if you can overlook the ghastly cartoons with which it is illustrated and interpret the rather garbled presentation, is the *RCAF 5BX Plan for Physical Fitness*.This program has been upstaged recently by the U.S. Air Force system of aerobics, a variety of exercises, like jogging, that stimulate heart and lung activity for a period long enough to produce lasting results. But the 5BX Plan is still valuable, either by itself or as complement to aerobics. You can buy the 5BX Plan at any government bookstore. There's another for women, the XBX Plan. These exercises, which are given for age groups up to fifty to sixty years, lead you gently through a system of carefully designed exercises, arranged so that you can take the course at your own rate without getting stiff and sore muscles.

Apart from important, specific matters of health, being in good shape contributes enormously to mental alertness, a sense of well-being, release from tension, in other words, enjoyment of life. One of the best exercises of all – probably *the* best of any single activity – is walking. (Don't believe those stories about it not taking off weight: all other things being equal, you can lose ten pounds a year by walking a mile a day.)

My own father, who was going downtown to lunch by himself when he was ninety-five, was a walker from as far back as I can remember. He had an easy, slow, rolling gait, rarely rode a bus or streetcar, and was one of the healthiest men, physically and mentally, I've ever known (he died at 95, from a fall on ice while out getting himself a dozen pints of beer). He loved his work of jewellery repairs, which he kept doing for fifteen years after his compulsory retirement, although I never heard him use the word "retired" in my life. He got a bit short of work at eighty-five but in his mind he hadn't retired from anything.

"Husbands will watch wives do the ironing, dust, vacuum, shop, salt the soup. . . ."

CHAPTER 12: LIVING AT HOME

There will be things to cope with at retirement, for both men and women. Wives are going to see more of their husbands around the house than they ever dreamt of in their worst nightmares as brides, and married couples might be surprised, at an age usually depicted on wedding-anniversary cards by two people beaming and rosy-cheeked and white-haired and surrounded by foot warmers and tea cosies and pipe racks, to find themselves looking up the office hours of marriage counsellors, or lawyers.

Some of the happiest marriages are that way because the husband and wife rarely see one another. For ten hours one is either downtown or on his way there or back and the other is at home; and for another eight they're both asleep, and the rest of the time they overlook the fact that they can barely communicate, and don't know what the other means when they do. There are romantic women who want to live on cliffs on stormy seacoasts, sprayed by salt, with shawls streaming out straight in a gale, in an atmosphere of kelp and high drama and tattered clouds drifting across the face of a full moon, married to men whose idea of drama is getting a fifteen per cent mark-up on power mowers and who think cliffs are risky investments; vague, pretty women who can spend $150 on a week's groceries without remembering how, and only vaguely aware of where, married to men who are always ruling sheets of paper trying to arrive at some systematic way of handling household expenses: and, what is a lot more common, men who live in a lofty world of jargon about financial affairs married to realtistic women who face inflation and have to make ends meet at the level of supermarket shelves. Most men haven't the faintest idea what goes on around the house, what women do, or what food costs. A woman I interviewed on inflation put it neatly when she said, "Let's face it, a man comes home and sees that everybody is alive and nothing is blocking the toilet and he thinks everything is okay."

Now they'll both be there facing each other at breakfast and supper unless at least one makes plans to get out of the house. A man's projects will start to sprawl over the kitchen drainboard. This causes fights and sometimes all hell will break loose in the golden years. While a man's wife will be sick of having him around, he will miss going downtown and will sit around watching Julia Child demonstrate how to make prune cakes instead of going out to those jolly, wet businessmen's luncheons. He'll be able to stand just so much time around the house, yet if he goes out without having to, his wife will begin to wonder whether he mightn't have something stashed away downtown, like a loose grandmother.

In fact, his wife will find the whole thing hard to understand, because she isn't retired. A woman never retires. A husband and wife will make little remarks to one another around the house like, "Well, I guess I'll go and clean my teeth." Husbands will watch wives do the ironing, dust, vacuum, shop, salt the soup, put inner linings in dresses, pink seams, and file their nails. Husbands will be there for try-ons at ten in the morning and be asked their opinions about dresses.

"I want an honest opinion. No, I mean it. Tell me exactly what you think of it."

"I like it."

"No I mean really. I don't want you to just say you like it when you don't. You don't have to worry about hurting my feelings."

"I'm telling you, it's – a nice dress. Honest, I like it."

"Tell me the *honest* truth."

"Well, I *like* it – but, I mean, I wouldn't mind if you hadn't told me you spent three months making it, but it kind of sags on top and it's too yellow."

"THANKS VERY MUCH! YOU SURE KNOW HOW TO MAKE A WOMAN FEEL GOOD."

With retirement, and relative freedom to move around, wives may start needling husbands to do things they don't want to do, and go places they don't want to go. Women are chronically restless, and the philosophy that things will be better somewhere else is strong in wives. It's one of the paradoxes of mankind that it was women who, before written history, induced their nomadic mates to stay in one place by planting snatch crops, yet women have been trying to get their husbands to go somewhere ever since 1841, when Thomas Cook, a Derbyshire teetotaller and temperance worker, began arranging tours to his bible meetings for people of ordinary means, to the disgust of the "in" travellers of the day.

Women are chronically restless. What a woman really wants is another husband, who she is convinced would be better than the one she has, but she's too loyal to say so, so she just tries to talk her husband into moving, to Australia, or Japan, or California, or the next street, or anywhere but where they are. All of which may be a good thing. It probably prevents the petrification of men over fifty and may account for the strange fact that there are more bright old ladies than bright old men. They're often travelling, with blue hair and all their buttons, asking if that's a stretch jet to Barcelona and sitting in places like the Plaka saying they'll just try another touch of that white stuff that smells like licorice.

A working woman who has retired will have a double problem: her own retirement, with all the changes it involves, and having a retired husband around expecting to be looked after. Men have a tendency to lean on women from everything from food to finding lost books. Agnes Macphail, Canada's first woman Member of Parliament, who sounded some historic bugle calls for women's rights, said, "My own father was a dear fellow, but I don't think he ever in his life found his shirt and his studs at the same time. What are these men that they can't take care of themselves? Babies in arms?"

MALE HECKLER: Don't you wish you were a man, Agnes?

AGNES: Yes, don't you?

Retirement, in short, means making important adjustments. Some of the adjustments should have been made years ago.

"Some of the greatest and most productive activity of man has been carried on in outward calm and quiet."

CHAPTER 13:
INTERESTS

In this book, it has been pointed out that it's foolish to think of retirement as a kind of misfortune. Mankind, back through the ages, would have thought of it as a stroke of unbelievable good luck.

For people who have been waiting for retirement in order to start some specific project – a second career – there's no problem of its being a psychological shock. They are just waiting to escape to a better life, often escape from dismal places of daily toil: warrens of offices in old buildings with creaking floors; new buildings of glass and plastic that have all the charm of a bathtub; machine shops with windows smeared with apricot paint to keep the sun out; gritty garages and those gritty little jokes workmates have been making for twenty-five years with the girls from the office, "Hey Norma, you need a tune-up?"

For those who aren't so clear about what they want to do when they retire, there are many new fields to look into, in business, politics, social service, conservation, study, crafts.

One ingenious idea that's catching on is a government-supported foreign-aid organization called Canadian Executive Service Overseas which finds jobs for retired businessmen and technicians, chiefly sixty and over. They and their wives are sent on six months of foreign service with no salary but travel and living expenses paid. They're briefed on the countries' politics, economics, and customs. Living quarters are located, the applicant is met in the new country and his wife introduced around. The "help wanted" bulletins sound mighty exciting: consultant on plastic footwear production for Cyprus; plant designer for Santa Angelo; geologist to organize exploration program in Iran. The literature lists some of the people who have been placed: a Kruger Pulp and Paper ex vice-president went to a paper mill in Pindamonhangaba, Brazil; a former Niagara Peninsula dry-cleaning and laundry executive found people glad of his help in Nairobi, Kenya; a former managing editor of the Vancouver *Sun* went to Nigeria to help a newspaper get on its feet; a T. Eaton Company general manager reorganized a dry-goods and hardware store in St. Lucia, West Indies; an ex vice-president of Green Giant went to Tanzania to advise on agriculture. Complete information on these jobs is available from Canadian Executive Service Overseas, 1010 St. Catherine Street West, Montreal.

But underlying the concrete details of any retirement plan is one essential idea: successful life isn't a matter of chronological age, but of interest in life. There's no reason for anyone to be bored. There's no reason not to be busy and active. But it's important to realize that this doesn't necessarily mean bustle and club joining and forced activity and compulsive front-lawn weeding. Some of the greatest and most productive activity of man has been carried on in outward calm and quiet. Gilbert White, one of the world's great naturalists, couldn't have looked very busy when he was making observations that he later recorded in *The Natural History of Selborne*: "This bird is most punctual in beginning its song exactly at the close of day; so exactly that I have known it strike up more than once or twice just at the report of the Portsmouth evening gun, which we can hear when the weather is still...."

Most of the mysteries of life are lying right before us. Henri Fabre, who wrote some of the best accounts of insect life ever published wrote, "And then, at last, my wish was fulfilled. I obtained a bit of land in the solitude of a little village. It was a *harmas*, which is the name we give in this part of Provence to an untilled, pebbly expanse where hardly any plant but thyme can grow ... there were plenty of weeds, couch grass and prickly centauries and the fierce Spanish oyster-plant with its spreading orange flowers and spikes strong as nails ... Such was the Eden that I won by forty years of desperate struggle ... Never have I seen so large a population of insects at a single spot. All the trades have made it their center. Here come hunters of every kinds of game, builders in clay, cotton weavers, leaf cutters, architects in pasteboard, plasterers mixing mortar, carpenters boring wood, miners digging underground galleries, workers in gold, beaters of skins and many more."

William James wrote in an essay called *On a Certain Blindness in Human Beings*: "Wherever a process of life communicates an eagerness to him who lives it, there the life becomes genuinely significant. Sometimes the eagerness is more knit up with the motor activities, sometimes with the perceptions, sometimes with the imagination, sometimes with reflective thought. But, wherever it is found, there is the zest, the tingle, the excitement of reality; and there *is* "importance" in the only real and positive sense in which importance ever anywhere can be."

There's no such thing as boredom: there's only frustration; and one of the great things about retirement is that you can plot your own course and you don't have to be frustrated any more. You can take a crack at all the things you've always wanted to do; and a lot you've probably never dreamt of. Every subject comes to life if you dig into it. I researched an article on the earthworm once and got so fascinated I hated to drop it to go on making a living. The worm is one of the strongest animals alive. He can move a rock sixty times his weight, and he eats stones to grind up his food. He was described by Aristotle and can grow to eleven feet in length. He eats dirt and excretes one of the most mysterious substances known to man – humus – without which there'd be no television or computers because there would be no men to invent them. All life is rooted in humus, or topsoil. Charles Darwin said of the worm, "It may be doubted whether there are many other animals which have played so important a part in the history of the world."

There are home-study books by top-flight people in just about every field you might be interested in; and there are all kinds of classes in high-school night courses and university extension courses – in French, anthropology, history, mathematics, art, physics, chemistry. I joined an evening chemistry class one time, and it was one of the most fascinating periods of my life – full of explosions and the sounds of bursting test tubes and breaking glassware and a noisy, red-headed teacher stained with chemicals shouting at us and the feeling that you were back in the mainstream of man's knowledge. There are ornithology and biology, astronomy and the making of sun dials and home telescopes. There are forestry and sociology and geology. Anybody who can't get interested in geology is a dull clod and deserves to spend the rest of his life playing shuffleboard. And it's a study that can be pursued anywhere. Torontonians, for instance, are sitting on and driving past some of the most famous ice-age deposits in the world, for the most part completely unaware of it.

With special low priced group fares and with the tourist industry thriving on people of average means, travel is available to most people now. The middle-aged today have an advantage, in a way, over the young, who are all going to Europe the way we used to go for Sunday drives. For anyone who hasn't been to Europe, the South Seas, Mexico, South America, or the Rockies or Prince Edward Island or Montreal or the prairies, will get that much more enjoyment out of it from having waited so long. You may not be able to sit up all night in a train without looking as if you'd been pole-axed, and stewardesses may tend to cluck over you when you spill your drinks, and you may be so slow making change in foreign currency that you'll drive Italian porters mad and they'll tear up tickets in your face and jump up and down on the pieces, but you'll enjoy travel all the more seeing things for the first time. I didn't see Europe until my mid-fifties and I've never experienced any emotion like the one I felt when, after sitting up all night across the Atlantic, I saw a distant necklace of orange-coloured sodium street lights gliding out from under the wing of a Boeing 707 somewhere over Scotland and realized that I was actually looking down on the land that had been part of my life since I was a schoolkid looking at Jeffery's line-drawings of Druids and Saxons and Danes and Norman knights. At dawn of the first day in London I heard horses hooves on pavement, a sound I hadn't heard since the bread wagons went up my street when I was a boy. When I pulled back the curtains of my hotel room window I saw a fierce snarling stone lion silhouetted against a murky pale yellow sky, and riding along the street below, helmeted guards in red coats. I had the feeling that I'd imagined a world of satellites and jets and moon walks and that this was the real world and that I'd just been having a kind of science-fiction dream.

Retirement now means a chance to take a new look at a world that is changed and changing, but still the same. Cities make the same roar in the distance as when you first listened to Mugsey Spanier; pigeons make the same soft racatacoo on warm downtown window ledges; the seeds of cottonwoods float down over sandy beaches; the summer countryside smells of buckwheat clover; hollyhocks still peer over brick walls; the bare branches of elms make the same beautiful patterns against the winter sky. A walk is still as enjoyable and full of fascinating sights as it was when you and your childhood pals used to go for those long Saturday hikes, down cliffs, along shores, up country roads, and along city streets, through burdock, thistle, and pickle factory shipping yards; when the gang would straggle home looking like Napoleon's retreat from Moscow, and exhaustion had focused all your senses till you just peered down at your moving feet, thinking what funny things they were, like ten inches of your leg turned up; still a bit dazed by all the wonderful things you'd seen of this world, and the even more wonderful things you were going to see tomorrow. That world hasn't changed. It's still there, waiting for you when you retire.

The following is a list of private organizations and government departments that offer a wealth of information which is free for the asking. Don't be hesitant about writing these people: if they can't be of assistance they will refer your request to the appropriate agency.

HEALTH AND WELFARE

ALBERTA
Alberta Department of Health,
Legislative Building,
Edmonton, Alberta

BRITISH COLUMBIA
British Columbia Department of Health Services
and Hospital Insurance,
Parliament Buildings,
Victoria, British Columbia

British Columbia Department of Rehabilitation
and Social Improvement,
Division of Aging,
411 Dunsmuir Street,
Vancouver 3, British Columbia

MANITOBA
Department of Health and Social Development,
Legislative Building,
Winnipeg, Manitoba

NEW BRUNSWICK
Department of Health and Welfare,
Legislative Building,
Fredericton, New Brunswick

NEWFOUNDLAND
Department of Health,
Confederation Building,
St. John's, Newfoundland

Department of Public Welfare,
Confederation Building,
St. John's, Newfoundland

NOVA SCOTIA
Department of Public Health,
Province House,
Halifax, Nova Scotia

Department of Public Welfare,
Province House,
Halifax, Nova Scotia

ONTARIO
> Department of Health,
> Hepburn Block,
> Parliament Buildings,
> Toronto, Ontario

> Department of Social and Family Services,
> Hepburn Block, Parliament Buildings,
> Toronto, Ontario

PRINCE EDWARD ISLAND
> Department of Health,
> Province House,
> Charlottetown, P.E.I.

> Department of Welfare,
> Province House,
> Charlottetown, P.E.I.

QUEBEC
> Department of Health,
> Parliament Buildings,
> Quebec, Quebec

> Department of Family and Social Welfare,
> 1075 Ste-Foy Road,
> Quebec, Quebec

SASKATCHEWAN
> Department of Public Health,
> Legislative Buildings,
> Regina, Saskatchewan

> Department of Welfare,
> Legislative Buildings,
> Regina, Saskatchewan

LIFE INSURANCE
>Canadian Life Insurance Association,
>44 King Street West,
>Toronto 1, Ontario

GENERAL INSURANCE
>Insurance Bureau of Canada,
>170 University Avenue,
>Toronto 110, Ontario

OLD AGE AND CANADA PENSION, GUARANTEED INCOME SUPPLEMENT
>Income Security Branch,
>Department of National Health and Welfare,
>Ottawa, Ontario

EMPLOYMENT
>Canadian Executive Service Overseas,
>1010 St. Catherine Street West,
>Montreal, Quebec
>
>Your local Canada Manpower branch
>
>"How to Run a Business," a booklet available for 75¢ from: Information Canada Bookstore, 171 Slater Street, Ottawa, Ontario

PROTECTION
>Legal Aid: see telephone directory
>
>Consumers Association of Canada,
>100 Gloucester Street,
>Ottawa 4, Ontario

Information and Public Relations Branch,
Department of Consumer and Corporate Affairs,
Canadian Building,
219 Laurier Avenue West,
Ottawa 4, Ontario

MOVING OR TOURING

The following government embassies in Ottawa may be able to help you directly, or they can put you in touch with an office in your area.

Embassy of Italy
172 MacLean Street,
Ottawa, Ontario

Embassy of Jamaica
85 Range Road,
Ottawa, Ontario

Embassy of Mexico
88 Metcalfe Street,
Ottawa, Ontario

Embassy of Spain
124 Springfield Road,
Ottawa, Ontario

United States Embassy
100 Wellington Street,
Ottawa, Ontario

Canadian Government Travel Bureau,
Department of Industry Trade and Commerce,
Ottawa, Ontario